THOUGHTS FROM THE MOUND

52 REFLECTIONS ON THE CHRISTIAN LIFE

Jeff A. Jenkins

ISBN-10: 0615875645
ISBN-13: 978-0615875644

Library of Congress Control Number: 2013956971

Published by Start2Finish Books
PO Box 660675 #54705
Dallas, TX 75266-0675
www.start2finish.org

Printed in the United States of America

Cover Design: Chad Landman

DEDICATION

to Laura

Other than the love of God, the love and commitment you
have shared with me is the greatest blessing in my life. You are
the model preacher's wife. You have never craved the limelight
or had a desire to make yourself famous. Thank you for standing
beside me through good days and bad. You are the love of my
life, and I am eternally thankful for all that you do, as well as all
that you are for the Lord. ILYFAF!

to Amanda & Jeremy

You are the two greatest gifts God has ever given us. My prayer
is that the words written in this book will strengthen your faith
and encourage you in your walk with God. My most sincere
prayer is that we will spend eternity together with our Lord.

to Evie, Ever, & Daniel

Our great God knew exactly when we needed you most in our
lives. We can't describe the joy you bring us. We pray every day that
you will grow up to be faithful Christians, and that you will marry
faithful Christians who will help you get to heaven. We pray that
your lives will be filled with joy, peace, and happiness.

CONTENTS

FOREWORD

David had Jonathan. Timothy had Paul. Jesus had John. And I have Jeff. Growing up, Jeff was always older than he should have been. Some would call it maturity. All I knew was that he lived upstairs and had friends who drove, that he dated early and was preaching by the time I was about two. He played tennis, golf, was point guard on his basketball team and quarterback on his football team. He was that guy who never did wrong, and who I didn't really know, but idolized.

I still have a postcard he sent me from New Orleans when I was 14 or 15. Even now, I can almost quote it. It was an outside shot of the then-new Superdome, and on it he wrote: "Wouldn't it be great to preach someday to this many people?" I remember thinking he probably would—and by now, he probably has.

When I went off to college, he was the big man on campus, and I was his little brother. He wrote me a note, and I kept it. When I graduated from college and began preaching, he was asked to hold a meeting in Pana, Illinois. He agreed on the condition that he could bring his kid brother with him, and we could share the preaching. And they did, and he did, and I did. He doesn't know it, but that trip changed my life as much as anything I ever remember. We talked, he shared, and I learned that we had the same positive passions and views on most everything. For the first time in my life, I felt not-so-strange. If one of my most significant heroes held these views, then I must be all right. I was also introduced to my first hot tub on that trip, and that changed me to—

But that's another story for another day.

Thus began something special that I have enjoyed for nearly three decades. Traveling with Jeff—gospel meetings, lectureships, family vacations, The Jenkins Institute webinars—each one wonderful by themselves, but were made monumental in that I got to pick Jeff's brain and enjoy his company. I got to be with my brother.

I remember when the e-mail popped up that Jeff had started a blog. My writing is rather rough, hard to untangle, a little raw, and sometimes seems to not know where it's going. Jeff's writing is, like him, disciplined and thoughtful. The best word I can use is strong. When I saw him blogging, I almost stopped because he is so powerful and complete in his writing.

Then came the request three months and one week after dad died. He suggested we combine our blogs into one site. I was very hesitant. I didn't want him to be pulled down by my silliness or have baggage as a result of what I might write. But he insisted he wanted to, and before that week of Freed-Hardeman Lectures was over, The Jenkins Institute was born. What a blessing it has been to me to get to work on this project, to continue our dad's work with him.

Jeff is funny about this. He will not like this honor, but he deserves it. Jeff is my hero, and I get to share him with a thankful brotherhood. Thank you, Jeff, for allowing God to use you to be a blessing. Thank you, reader, for taking the time to consider these posts.

Your life will be richer for it.

— Dale Jenkins
Spring Hill, Tennessee

INTRODUCTION

Our home is in Flower Mound, Texas, located northwest of Dallas. Even though the population is quickly approaching 70,000, it is still known as "The Town of Flower Mound." Flower Mound derives its name from a literal flower mound that rises 650 feet above sea level and stands 50 feet above the surrounding countryside. Our house is located approximately five miles north of this historic mound of flowers! We have loved every place we have ever lived, but we love Flower Mound the most.

When I made the decision a few years ago to enter the blogosphere, we decided to name the blog "Thoughts From the Mound." Most of the articles in this book were written in our home. From the beginning of the blog, it has been our goal that these posts would encourage those who read them to be drawn closer to Jesus.

You will notice that these articles are not primarily doctrinal in nature. You will find some doctrinal information in these pages, but the focus is on the devotional rather than the doctrinal. My most sincere prayer is that these articles will help all of us as we seek to glorify God in all we do, in all we think, and in all we say.

If you would like to read more articles like these, you can find them in abundance at thejenkinsinstitute.com.

JESUS IS LORD

December 13, 2012

The all-consuming goal in the life of Paul was to know Jesus and to become more like him. In his letter to the Philippian Christians, Paul explains the goal. "That I may know him and the power of his resurrection, and may share his sufferings, becoming like him in his death" (Phil. 3:10). Paul was well aware that he had not yet reached the goal, yet he was always striving (Phil. 3:12).

If Jesus is truly Lord of our life, and if we are his subjects, this will be our goal as well. When the New Testament speaks of becoming more like Christ, it employs words like sanctification and holiness. Certainly every child of God knows the importance of holiness, and all of us want to be holy. The question is, how are we to become more holy? How can we become more like Jesus? In Phil. 3, Paul helps us with this. He admonishes his readers in three areas.

1. Leave the past behind. Paul begins by telling us that if we are going to become more like Jesus we must let go of the past. "Brothers, I do not consider that I have made it my own. But one thing I do: forgetting what lies behind and straining forward to what lies ahead" (Phil. 3:13). We must be willing to leave sin behind. We can never become all that God wants us to be if we continue living in sin. Paul would say to the Romans that we must seek to rid our lives of sin

(Rom. 6:11–15). We must put off the old man and put on the new (Eph. 4:22, Col. 3:9).

We must also be willing to leave the guilt of sin behind. One of the reasons so many Christians struggle is that they are not certain of their salvation. They don't feel forgiven. When our God forgives, he forgets.

Think about the terminology Scripture uses to describe God's forgiveness. "You have cast all my sins behind your back" (Isa. 38:17). "You will cast all our sins into the depths of the sea" (Mic. 7:19). "As far as the east is from the west, so far does he remove our transgressions from us" (Psa. 103:12). "Come now, let us reason together, says the LORD: though your sins are like scarlet, they shall be as white as snow; though they are red like crimson, they shall become like wool" (Isa. 1:18).

Our God is described as the forgiving God who abundantly pardons (Mic. 7:18; Psa. 103:3). The more we learn about God, the more we will learn the meaning of forgiveness. The more we learn about God, the more we will be able to know we are truly forgiven.

One additional thought about leaving the past behind. If we are going to be able to grow in our faith and become more like Jesus, we cannot dwell on our past accomplishments. Many Christians live in the past and believe they can rest on their own past, as well as the past of others. "My parents were such good Christians. When I was growing up, I never missed church. I used to be committed to Christ, but my life has changed." In the early part of Phil. 3, Paul discusses his heritage and his past. "Though I myself have reason for confidence in the flesh also. If anyone else thinks he has reason for confidence in the flesh, I have more: circumcised on the eighth day, of the people of Israel, of the tribe of Benjamin, a Hebrew of Hebrews; as to the law, a Pharisee; as to zeal, a persecutor of the church; as to righteousness under the law, blameless" (Phil. 3:4–6).

However, notice how Paul says he felt about all of his past

accomplishments after meeting Jesus. "But whatever gain I had, I counted as loss for the sake of Christ. Indeed, I count everything as loss because of the surpassing worth of knowing Christ Jesus my Lord" (Phil. 3:7–8).

2. Lean on proper examples. We must lean on the right examples. In this text, Paul speaks of this idea both negatively and positively. There are some things, as well as some people, in this life that Christians need to flee. "For many, of whom I have often told you and now tell you even with tears, walk as enemies of the cross of Christ. Their end is destruction, their god is their belly, and they glory in their shame, with minds set on earthly things" (Phil. 3:18-19). Peter reminds Christians "to abstain from the passions of the flesh, which wage war against your soul" (1 Pet. 2:11).

On the positive side, there are many wonderful examples we can follow. "Brothers, join in imitating me, and keep your eyes on those who walk according to the example you have in us" (Phil. 3:17). Not because any of these people are perfect, but because they have proven themselves to be faithful.

Paul also said, "Be imitators of me, as I am of Christ" (1 Cor. 11:1). Only those who are seeking to follow Christ are worthy of our imitation. We would all do well to find people who have lived godly lives, so that we can imitate them as we walk through our own life.

3. Look to the prize. We must look to the future. It's not enough to forget the past. We must also focus on the future—the eternal future. Where we are going to spend eternity should be the highest priority in our lives. What matters most in this life is not how far we climb up the corporate ladder, or how much money we make. It is not what kind of car we have, or how big our house is. What matters most is our eternal destiny. Where will we spend eternity?

Paul speaks clearly, "But our citizenship is in heaven, and from it we await a Savior, the Lord Jesus Christ, who will transform our lowly body to be like his glorious body, by the power that enables him even to subject all things to himself" (Phil. 3:20–21).

The word Paul uses here for citizenship is similar to our word politics. Paul is saying that, regardless of where we live, regardless of who rules over us here on this earth, our government is in heaven. We always follow God rather than man! We are strangers and pilgrims on this earth (1 Pet. 2:11; Heb. 11:13). Like those faithful saints of old, we are looking for a better place: our homeland (Heb. 11:14).

As long as we are here, "we await a Savior, the Lord Jesus Christ" (Phil. 3:20). Jesus has prepared a place for those who will become and live as his subjects (John 14:1–3). When Jesus comes again in the clouds, he will take us home to live with him (1 Thess. 4:16–17).

We seek to follow him, to become more like him, to be sanctified and holy. If we remain faithful in our lives, he "will transform our lowly body to be like his glorious body" (Phil. 3:21). What we spend our entire lives seeking will be bestowed upon us by a loving Savior. The goal of every child of God will become the prize received by those who are faithful to Him. Praise God for the help of Jesus in being victorious!

Dear Father in heaven, we thank you for our salvation that comes through Jesus. We pray that we will strive every day to become more like him. We pray that we will grow in our relationship with him, and that we will become stronger in our faith. Help us, dear God, to show those around us what it means to have Christ in us. In Jesus' name, Amen.

WHAT IS YOUR MINISTRY?

March 7, 2010

A close preacher-friend was telling me recently about a sister he knew who made homemade pies for every man in the church on his birthday. One year, she made pies on 220 days—that's a lot of pies! She explained that it was her ministry. It caused me to think about all those I've known through the years who minister to others.

In Eph. 4, Paul speaks of equipping the saints for ministry. We sometimes have the misguided idea that ministry is only for professionals, i.e. the paid guys. But the truth is that ministry is for everyone. The verb "to minister" comes from a Greek word (*diakoneo*), meaning to serve. The noun, "minister" (from the Greek *diakonos*) means servant or minister. Jesus made it very clear that anyone who wants to be great must be a minister (Matt. 20:26). Then our Lord began teaching his followers how to serve one another (John 13). Our Lord performed the ultimate act of ministry when he gave himself on the cross for us (Mark 10:45). If we wish to be like him, we will be willing to give of ourselves to others (Phil. 2:5–8).

I remember seeing a church sign several years ago that said, "Minister – Every Member." If every Christian is ministering to others, all of God's people will have what they need most. It has been my experience over the years that I am happiest when I am serving others. It has also been my experience that those who are busy serving others are the least likely to complain. Servants are those most likely to be evangelistic.

Please allow me to share a few personal ministries I am aware of in hopes it might encourage others to find their own ministry.

- *The Bicycle Recycle Ministry.* A brother noticed he had several bicycles in his garage that were not being used, so he cleaned them up, tuned them up, and gave them away to homeless people with no transportation. He started asking around and learned that there were many others who were in the same situation. People everywhere started bringing him bikes. Organizations have collected bikes for him. He now has given hundreds, perhaps thousands, of bikes to people who are on foot.

- *The Calling Ministry.* We have a sister who attempts to make a personal phone call to every visitor who comes to our worship services. She gives each of them a warm welcome, learns what she can about their background, and brags about the church. She has arranged numerous Bible studies, and I am convinced a number of people will be in heaven because of her ministry.

- *The Email Ministry.* One of our elders emails every visitor who attends our services. He lets them know how glad we were to have them with us. He invites them back again, and he tells them he will be glad to answer any questions they might have about the church.

- *The Mowing Ministry.* I knew a man who would take his son and mow yards for elderly and shut-in folks who couldn't do it themselves. He never charged them a dime and in the process he taught his son how to serve others.

- *The Prayer-Chain Ministry.* We have a handful of

sisters who keep a running list of church members, as well as family and friends of church members, who need special prayers. They print a new list for distribution every time we gather. These sisters make calls or send emails to our elders and preachers to update us on those who need prayers. They also have emergency prayer-calls when needed.

- *The Can Ministry.* A brother collects cans, sells them to be recycled, then gives the money to children's homes. Over the years, thousands of dollars have been given to homes that have blessed the lives of countless children.

- *The Children's Home Ministry.* Two teams of ladies go to a local children's home each week to help however they are needed. They work primarily in getting clothes ready to sell to raise money for the home. One of the sisters picks up bread from a local restaurant at the end of the day to take with them to the children's home to be divided among the different houses.

- *The Pillow Ministry.* We have a group that meets in our building each week to make pillows that are taken to local hospitals. They stitch the name and address of the church on the pillow to let the recipients know the church loves them.

None of these people care if anybody knows their names. They don't do this work to be praised or recognized, but because they want to be the arms, hands, feet, and hearts of Jesus. They want others to know about the love of the Lord.

During the past thirty years of preaching, I have occasionally heard someone ridicule the church for being unloving, uncaring, or unsympathetic. Some will say Christians are only interested in doctrine, numbers, money, etc. But my experience has been that this type of statement is a smokescreen. People usually speak this way when they are angry, they don't like something, or they want the church to change. The Christians I have known in my life are the most loving, charitable, caring people in the world.

I have only highlighted a few of many, many ministries. I know those who have given up their vacation time for mission trips, youth trips, work camps, etc. I know families who have worked in food kitchens. I know Christians who have gone to help out with cleanup after a natural disaster, both locally and abroad. I know others who have anonymously supported worthy causes.

Dear God, thank you for so many wonderful Christians who give of their time, money, and talent to help others. Thank you for those who are so unselfish and who seek no personal glory. Thank you, Father, for the many doors of opportunity you open for us. Help us, dear Lord, to do as much good, for as many possible, as long as we can. Help us to have the heart of a servant. Help us to be more like Jesus every day. In Jesus' name, Amen.

REASON FOR HOPE

November 2, 2009

While discussing the work of the church over lunch the other day with a retired preacher, our conversation turned as it often does to friends in other places. We started talking about two dear sisters whom we both love deeply, who have had Alzheimer's disease. One recently lost her life and another is currently struggling with this horrible disease. My friend made the comment that just about everybody he knows who has been affected by Alzheimer's is an individual who is highly organized. We both sort of smiled and agreed that, if that is the case, neither of us has anything to worry about. I told him his comment gave me a lot of hope. As I was driving away that day I began to think about hope.

In our finite minds, it is difficult for us to understand the real meaning of hope. We use hope every day in our vocabulary. We use hope to represent something we want to happen, but something of which we are really uncertain. For example, there are many of us who hope the Dallas Cowboys can win a playoff game this year. We don't feel very confident in this, but we hope it will happen! A child may say, "I hope I get a new doll or a new game for Christmas." We may hope for a new job, a new house, or a new car. To us, hope is represented by strong desire, but not much more.

The biblical idea of hope is much different. In the Bible, hope represents something more substantive than desire. Hope in the Bible is accompanied more with assurance. The apostle Paul gives us the best biblical definition of hope in Rom. 8:24–25, "For in this hope we were saved. Now hope that is seen is not hope. For who hopes for what he sees? But if we hope for what we do not see, we wait for it with patience."

This passage gives us something we believe in, not something about which we are uncertain. Paul would later say we should rejoice in this hope (Rom. 12:12). It is "through endurance and through the encouragement of the Scriptures" that we gain this hope (Rom. 15:4). There is one hope in which we have been called as Christians (Eph. 4:4). The writer of Hebrews reminds us that our hope is both "sure and steadfast," that it serves as an "anchor of the soul" (Heb. 6:19).

We hope in the gospel. We live in a world that is hopelessly lost. However, there is Good News. Jesus came into the world to save the lost (Luke 19:10). Our hope is not in ourselves, our own ingenuity, our own educational acumen, our own planning—our hope is in the gospel. The apostle Paul spoke of the hope of the gospel that the early Christians had heard, and reminded all of us that this is our "hope of glory" (Col. 1:23, 27). Once we have obeyed this gospel, we have put on the "hope of salvation" (1 Thess. 5:8). When we are born again, we have a "living hope" (1 Pet. 1:3). We must be willing to help others learn of this great hope. It is true that Christianity can be characterized as one beggar helping another beggar find bread. The words of Paul in 1 Tim. 4:10 paint a clear picture of our work, "For to this end we toil and strive, because we have our hope set on the living God, who is the Savior of all people, especially of those who believe." When we share this hope with others, they become "our hope … before our Lord Jesus at his coming" (1 Thess. 2:19).

We hope in the coming of Jesus. In Acts 1, we read of Jesus going back to heaven to be with the Father. When Christ ascended, two men in white clothing appeared and said to the disciples who were gazing intently into the sky, "Men of Galilee, why do you stand looking into heaven? This Jesus, who was taken up from you into heaven, will come in the same way as you saw him go into heaven" (Acts 1:11). Jesus is coming back in the clouds, just as he ascended in the clouds, so that he might take us to live with him eternally (John 14:1–3). In Phil. 3:20–21, Paul stated that we eagerly await the coming of the Savior. Since the earliest days of Christianity, all Christians are "waiting for our blessed hope, the appearing of the glory of our great God and Savior Jesus Christ" (Titus 2:13). This is the hope that will help us live pure lives (1 John 3:3).

We hope in our eternal salvation. When the author of Hebrews states that we have this hope as an anchor of the soul, he is referring to our entrance into our eternal home. It is this hope that sustains the people of God. It is this hope that gives us reason to live faithfully for him. It is this hope that encourages us to want to share the hope of the gospel with others. This is the hope of eternal life, "which God, who never lies, promised before the ages began" (Tit. 1:2). Those who are justified have been made heirs of this hope (Titus 3:7). This hope is certain. It is not something we have to be unsure about; we can have the "full assurance of hope" (Heb. 6:11). This hope has been reserved for us in heaven (Col. 1:5).

Thank you, dear Father, for giving us the hope that is an anchor for our souls! Please help us to place our hope in you. In Jesus' name, Amen.

WHATEVER YOU DO

May 18, 2010

Recently while flying, three people were sitting behind me on the plane and talking very loudly. It was clearly obvious that neither of them liked their job very much. One of the individuals was especially annoying. He droned on incessantly about all of the projects he was involved with. When the other started to speak, he interrupted with another story about himself. He was quite full of himself. The screaming baby in the seat behind me was actually a relief from the other noise!

Most people are not happy in their jobs. As a matter of fact, many people in America hate the work they do. I've personally talked with many people who would change jobs today if something else were available. But that happens to be one if the biggest problems—nothing else is available. In a recent survey from Adecco and Harris Interactive, "the majority of American workers say they plan to start looking for work when the economy recovers." Forbes magazine says five million Americans are out of work right now. The unemployment rate currently stands right at 10% according to the latest figures from the U. S. Bureau of Labor Statistics! So in this environment, what's a Christian to do? Please consider just a few thoughts.

If you have a job, thank God every day. Knowing how many people in our world who are without jobs should remind those of us who have them just how blessed we are. Even those who do not like their job are at least blessed with work. Pray every day! We should ask God to help us have the right attitude about our work. We should ask him to help us look at our work as a place to evangelize.

We are only here a short time. We are strangers and pilgrims on this earth. In that sense, all jobs are part-time. If you consider your work a trial, remember that Paul said, "For this light momentary affliction is preparing for us an eternal weight of glory beyond all comparison" (2 Cor. 4:17). We will not work forever.

Set the right example for others. We are to live our lives, even when unhappy at work, in such a way that those who work with us will not have reason to speak evil of us. Peter told the early Christians, "Keep your conduct among the Gentiles honorable, so that when they speak against you as evildoers, they may see your good deeds and glorify God on the day of visitation" (1 Pet. 2:12). The Lord is our ultimate judge and the one to whom we give glory! Remember that our Savior told us to let our lights shine before everyone around us so that our Father will be glorified (Matt. 5:14–16).

View your workplace as an opportunity to tell others about Jesus. Our primary job in this life is to help others find their way to heaven. We need to try to tell as many people as possible about Jesus (Matt. 28:18–20). We can win our friends, family and co-workers to Christ by the way we live our lives (1 Pet. 2:12; 3:1).

Plan for the future. This life is a training ground for heaven. We should always be working to better ourselves in this life. Whatever we do in this life should be done to bring glory to God (1 Cor. 10:31). We are looking toward a better city, an eternal home where we will rest forever (Heb. 11:16; 13:14).

Focus on what's most important. Family, spiritual growth, and church are all more important than our jobs. Some Christians are so into their work that they can't appreciate the most important aspects of life. We would probably all be happier if we kept our work in the right perspective. If we give priority to what God wants us to put first, we may enjoy our jobs more. Our job is not the most important part of our life. God wants us to work hard, but he has given us priorities that should receive more attention than the work we do. We should put more emphasis on our own spiritual growth than we do our job (1 Pet. 2:2; 2 Pet. 3:18; Heb. 5:12–14). Our eternal destination is more important than anything else in this life (Phil. 3:20–21). Our family should be more meaningful and important to us than our job. Paul said that husbands should love their wives in the way Christ loved the church, and that we should love our wives like we do our own bodies (Eph. 5:25, 28). Being the spiritual leader in our family is more important than any job we might have (Eph. 6:4).

Dear Father, we thank you for everything you have done for us. We thank you for the opportunity to glorify you in every part of our life. Help us, dear God, to constantly be aware of the fact that we live and work among people who do not know our Lord. Help us to tell them the Good News that can bring them salvation. Help us in our work to glorify you by our attitudes and conduct. We pray for those who do not have jobs and for those who are struggling in the job they have. May we always be concerned for others and may we always be thankful to you. In Jesus' name, Amen.

SHE GAVE AWAY BIBLES

May 20, 2010

Today, I had the privilege of baptizing a young lady named Jasmin into Christ for the remission of her sins. She is the third person we've baptized in the past few days. I am convinced that there is no greater joy in this life than seeing someone become a child of God. Allow me to tell you a little of Jasmin's story.

One of our dear ladies, Dorothy, was having a yard sale some time back. Whenever anyone came to her yard sale, she offered them a free Bible. What a tremendous idea! What if every Christian family who has a yard sale gave free Bibles to everyone who comes by?

Jasmin lives a couple of blocks away from Dorothy, and she was taking a walk that morning. Jasmin was raised in the Catholic church, and she stated that she had been questioning her teaching. She had even written some poems about what she felt was missing in her religion. As she walked that morning, she prayed that God would help her find someone who could assist her with her questions. She was surprised when she walked up to the yard sale and was offered a Bible. When she accepted, Dorothy asked her if she would like to have a Bible study. Jasmin said she would love to study. Over the next several weeks, the two ladies studied the Word of God together. Dorothy said that sometimes the studies lasted three hours at a time.

Jasmin was an eager learner. After the baptism today, we prayed together. After we prayed, Jasmin said, "I am so glad I met Dorothy, or I would still be lost." A few thoughts have come to mind as I have thanked God for our new sister in the Lord.

There are many ways to approach people who do not know Jesus. Free Bibles at a yard sale—what a tremendous way to get the Good News to people who may not know it! A dear sister who recently passed away always carried church business cards with her. She left them in restaurants, gave them to people at the grocery store, and even while in the hospital gave them to the hospital workers. She invited some of them to come to worship with her. Another sister I know conducts Bible studies every week at her business. She has had the opportunity to study with co-workers on numerous occasions. We need to be creative in the ways we approach people with the gospel.

You don't have to be a professional to lead someone to Jesus. In our day of professional vocation, we sometimes get the idea that only church leaders or paid staff members can teach the gospel. We could not be more mistaken. The gospel will be spread best when every child of God sees the importance of telling others. None of the ladies mentioned above are "professionals," but they all have a passion for sharing the Good News. Why not make a commitment to find a way to teach someone about Jesus before the end of the year? Imagine if everyone who reads this would convert one person this year!

People are searching. There are people in our area of influence who are searching for Jesus. We just have to keep looking. They are in our neighborhoods, in our schools, at our work, on our team, in the mall, on the golf course, at the park, and all around us. There are many Jasmin's who are sincerely looking for answers to life's questions. We don't have to be hard-nosed, mean-spirited, or arrogant. We just need to listen and look around us. There are many among us who would have never approached this young lady about a Bible study. Some because they don't believe it will work. Others refuse to tell others about Jesus because they are not willing to take the time. Some because they have convinced themselves that those who are already "churched" (part of a religious group) are saved and should be left alone. Jasmin said, "If I had not met Dorothy, I would still be lost." How interesting that she realized she was lost and needed to obey Christ, but some of God's people can't get that?

The gospel still saves. The apostle Paul said, "For I am not ashamed of the gospel, for it is the power of God for salvation" (Rom. 1:16). It is not our educational acumen, our ingenuity, our planning, our ideas, or our work that is the power of salvation. It is the gospel, the Good News about Jesus. Like Paul, we need to be eager at all times to teach it (Rom. 1:15). If we could develop the attitude portrayed in Gal. 6:14, we might be more willing to share the message, "But far be it from me to boast except in the cross of our Lord Jesus Christ." The message of salvation is clear and simple. When we believe that, and when we are willing to share it with others, we will see tremendous results.

Father, we give you thanks for Christians who are willing to share the Good News with others. We thank you for opening doors of opportunity for us to spread the Word. Dear God, we are thankful for people like Jasmin who are searching for answers, and we are thankful for people like Dorothy who are willing to take the time to lead someone else to you. Help us, dear Lord, to search for opportunities and to be creative in how we approach others. In Jesus' name, Amen.

THE LIGHT OF ALL MEN

May 2, 2013

It is natural for human beings to be interested in introductions. There are websites dedicated to helping speakers learn how to introduce speeches. The first readers of John's account of the gospel must have been struck with his introduction to the Gospel of John. Nearly 2,000 years later, the introduction continues to arrest our attention. It is designed to give the reader an exalted picture of the dignity of our Redeemer. It causes us to want to obey and love him even more. The introduction that John pens causes us to have great interest in the inspired account of Jesus!

His relationship to God. In these opening verses, John uses the word *logos*. While we understand *logos* to mean *word*, it also involves reasoning, specifically the mental faculty of thinking, meditating, reasoning, and calculating. John opens this book by describing the relationship between Jesus and the Father. In the first couple of verses we are reminded of some amazing facts about Jesus.

1. He was in the beginning with God. The Bible does not say he had a beginning, but that he was already there "in the beginning" before the creation occurred. This statement substantiates what we read in Gen. 1:26. "Let us make man in our image…

2. He was "with God." Jesus was in fellowship and relationship with the Father. The Scriptures show that he was equal with God, but "did not count equality with God a thing to be grasped, but emptied himself, by taking the form of a servant, being born in the likeness of men" (Phil. 2:6–7).

3. We see that "the Word was God." He possesses the characteristics of God, such as his eternal nature, identity, purpose, and mind. While Jesus certainly subjected himself to human limitations during his incarnation (Heb. 2:17, 18; 4:14–16), he did not become a different person. While on earth, he was still the eternal One (John 5:18; 8:56–59; 20:28).

John is making the undeniable claim that Jesus is deity (John 1:1–2). Many in the first century, as well as today, refused to accept this claim. John is telling us that Jesus is the very expression of God. He is God's communication to man (John 1:14).

His relationship to creation. In the next two verses (John 1:3–4), the apostle points out to his readers that Jesus was actively involved in creation. He tells us that there was nothing created without the Word; in fact, "all things were created by him." In the creation, we witness the power, majesty, and wisdom of God, the Word.

In addition to John's introduction, there are a number of other passages that clearly point to Jesus as being an active agent in creation. God created "all things" which he "carried out in Christ Jesus our Lord" (Eph. 3:9–11) Again speaking of the Son, "For by him all things were created, in heaven and on earth, visible and invisible, whether thrones or dominions or rulers or authorities—all things were created through him and for him. And he is before all things, and in him all things hold together" (Col. 1:16–17). "In these last days he has spoken to us by his Son, whom he appointed the heir of all things, through whom also he created the world" (Heb. 1:2; cf. 1:10–12).

These passages reiterate what John tells us in his introduction. Nothing has come into being apart from Jesus. This means that the Son himself is eternal, for he couldn't have created himself! He is the source of life itself.

His relationship to us. In the next few passages, John introduces his gospel by teaching us about the relationship that Jesus has with us. In explaining how Christ is in relationship to us, he describes how Jesus is light.

Jesus, the Life, became the Light of Men (John 1:4–5). The phrase "and the life was the light of men" is in the Greek imperfect tense. This means that "the life" began to be "the light of men" in the past and continues to be so in the present time. The Son of God is the source and essence of life itself. When lost in darkness and death, the best place to look for redemption is the source of all life—Jesus, the Son—and not the source of death—Satan, the adversary. "For the wages of sin is death, but the free gift of God is eternal life in Christ Jesus our Lord" (Rom. 6:23).

Even as the Son first gave physical life to the creatures of the world, and just as he continues to uphold "the universe by the word of his power" (Heb. 1:3), he offers spiritual life to the spiritually dead and eternal life to those who live by faith. In the darkness of suffering and sin, as evil and wickedness continue to have such a cruel impact on our existence in this world, it would seem as if people would be flocking to the light that has come into the world. But that is not the way it is! Those who live in darkness have great difficulty comprehending the light (John 1:5). In fact, there are many who hate the light, and when they hate the light, they cannot come to it (John 3:20).

In Scripture, light is often used in reference to knowledge. Notice just a few.

- "Blessed are the people who know the festal shout, who

walk, O LORD, in the light of your face" (Psa. 89:15).

- "For God, who said, 'Let light shine out of darkness,' has shone in our hearts to give the light of the knowledge of the glory of God in the face of Jesus Christ" (2 Cor. 4:6).

- "Having the eyes of your hearts enlightened, that you may know what is the hope to which he has called you, what are the riches of his glorious inheritance in the saints" (Eph. 1:18).

This Light is for every man. "The true light, which gives light to everyone, was coming into the world" (John 1:9). John reminds us that Jesus, the true light, came to save every man. God's message of love is for the entire world (John 3:16). He does not want anyone to perish (2 Pet. 3:9). The grace that brings light is made available to every person in the world. The question is, will we remain in darkness, or will we receive the life which is the light of men?

Dear Father in heaven, thank you for sending Jesus, the light of all men, into the world. Help us to take the light to everyone we come in contact with. Help us to allow our light to shine; help us, dear God, to be the light in a dark world. In Jesus' name, Amen.

THOUGHTS ON TRAGEDY

December 17, 2012

The collective heart of our nation was pierced this past weekend by the senseless murder of innocent children at Sandy Hook Elementary and the adults who cared for them. In our sorrow, we have seen the faces of these precious children who are now in the eternal presence of God. Better men have and will write their helpful thoughts about this tragedy. My prayer is that the following thoughts might bring some comfort and encouragement to those who read them.

Sinful acts always bring pain. Whenever someone commits a heinous, senseless act like taking the lives of innocent children, the pain seems unbearable. When we see the pain caused by sin, it may help us to consider our own sin. We hurt others when we sin. We hurt others with our actions. We hurt others with our words. We hurt family members, friends, fellow Christians, and people we don't even know.

A husband who walks out on his wife and children because he has found someone else brings great harm.

A mother who decides she no longer loves her husband brings great harm.

Parents who turn the raising of their children over to others just to build a better lifestyle harm their children greatly.

An adult child who turns his or her back on the teachings of their parents causes great pain.

A friend who turns their back on another friend, or spreads gossip about another friend, causes pain.

A Christian who says no to the Lord breaks the heart of the Savior.

Satan is alive and busy. In our fallen world, Satan "prowls around like a roaring lion, seeking someone to devour" (1 Pet 5:8). Satan can devour us when he tempts us and succeeds in getting us to turn away from God. Satan can devour us by getting us to turn our eyes away from our purpose to glorify God (1 Pet. 4:11). Satan can devour us by causing us to take our eyes off our mission to proclaim the Good News to the world (Matt. 28:18–20). Satan can devour us by discouraging us with the evil that exists in our world.

Some events don't make sense. We all want to know how something like this could happen. We want to know what in the world would cause an individual to decide to kill innocent children. We want to know why.

The unfortunate bottom line is there are some things that just don't make sense. There are no easy answers. We can know that as long as sinful men exist in a fallen world, sinful acts will occur. Sin causes us to do unspeakable things. Other senseless events that don't make sense have occurred in the past few days and will continue to occur.

We can also know that as long as Christians are in the world, good things will happen. People who have Christ living in them will comfort those who mourn. They will encourage the brokenhearted. They will reach out to the hurting with the love of Jesus.

Sorrow is a part of every life. Job said, "Man who is born of a woman is few of days and full of trouble" (Job 14:1). As long as this fallen world exists, there will be sorrow. The tears of life cannot be permanently wiped away until we enter into the eternal presence of God (Rev. 21:4).

There will be times in our life when we are on top of the mountain. There will also be times that we will find ourselves in the valley. The goal should be to eventually find our way out of the sorrowful moments and enjoy life to the best of our ability. No one who lives very long is immune to sorrow. We must all endure it to understand fully the joy that we can experience in Jesus.

Some things are better left unsaid. When we lost a son, a well-meaning sister came to the hospital to "cheer us up." She sat for what seemed like hours and told us jokes and what she thought were humorous stories. We were not amused.

Grief should not be rushed. Some people may get over a tragedy quickly, but most people take a lot of time to grieve. To try to rush someone through grief just because you were able to get through it quickly is thoughtless.

It is unconscionable how some folks use a tragedy like this to push their agenda. It took only a few minutes for those who want to outlaw guns to begin their campaign again. Some who call themselves Christians and despise the anti-gun crowd are using this platform to push that agenda fail to see the correlation when they use a tragedy like this to push their agenda. Some Christians are using this terrible event to advance their beliefs about abortion, praying in school, homeschooling, and elections.

It is wrong-headed thinking to try to convince ourselves or others that, if we would just outlaw guns, if we would just allow praying in school, if we would all homeschool our children, or if we would just elect the right government officials, then tragic events like this would never happen.

We must learn that, as long as evil exists, we will have to deal with unthinkable acts. They will happen in shopping malls, movie theaters, on street corners, in "safe" neighborhoods, and even church buildings. I have known preachers and elders who have abused children in the house of worship. These kinds of evil acts can happen anywhere when people choose to sin.

I am not saying we should never discuss the aforementioned topics; I'm just saying we need to be sensitive to those who are suffering and cease using their time of sorrow to advance our cause. The Holy Spirit was clear that there is a time when we should do and say what we think. By implication, he was also saying there are times we should refrain from doing and saying what we think (Eccl. 3:1-8).

A few years ago, some very dear friends of ours lost their son while he was protecting our nation. I cringed when I heard someone say in the presence of my friends that the Lord, through their prayers, had brought their loved one home safely. My friends were faithful in their walk with God, and they prayed every day that their son would come home safe. He did not. I will not discuss the theology of that entire thought here. I will simply say that we must be sensitive to the pain of others when we speak. Sometimes we need to hold our thoughts close to the vest.

Sensing God's presence is not always easy. One question often asked when a terrible tragedy such as this happens is, "Where was God?" We believe God is present in our world. However, God does not stop every tragedy. God allows human beings to make their own choices. And just as we are heartbroken when people we love make harmful choices, it breaks the heart of God to watch people he has created hurt others. God weeps when his people or when his little children are hurt. It is during those times when we have been hurt the deepest that we struggle with sensing the presence of God.

Think of Job when his family was being slaughtered by Satan— he lost ten children in one day. Think of Joseph being thrown into a pit by his brothers, then sold into slavery, then thrown into prison for thirteen years. Only after it all happened was he able to recognize fully that God had been with him through it all.

Think of the Son of God himself being suspended between heaven and earth, crying out, "My God, My God, why have you forsaken me? " There will always be dark moments when we have difficulty sensing the presence of our Father. Even when we cannot sense it, he is very near.

Sharing hope is crucial when tragedy strikes. My wife and I had a son who passed away after only living for about ten minutes. I lost both of my parents too soon. My wife has been through two bouts with cancer at a relatively early age. I have family members who have turned their back on the Lord and his church.

I know many have been through much worse in their life. I tell you this to simply say that a God of hope sustains us. Our Father promises that regardless of what we face in this life, if we will remain loyal to him, we will receive the crown of life (2 Tim. 4:7–8). It is this hope that motivates us to continue living for him. It is this hope that encourages us to remain faithful. It is this hope that children of the King must share with the world.

Jesus is the ultimate hope for our world, for our nation, for our families, for the church, and for our lives. Jesus is the message our world needs to hear. Not from smug, arrogant people who think they have arrived. But from broken, lost, hopeless people who have been redeemed and given a new, living hope (Eph. 1:18; Rom. 15:13; 1 Pet. 1:3).

Let us continue our prayers for those whose lives have forever been altered by this tragedy. Let us pray that they will find hope and peace in Jesus. Let us pray for the family of the man who committed this unspeakable act. Let us pray for our nation, that Jesus might be found again. Let us pray for our families, that Jesus might reign in our hearts. Let us pray for the church, that the compassion and love of Jesus might live within us.

Dear Father in Heaven, we continue to pray for the many families grieving because of the loss of their loved ones. We pray that they might find peace, comfort, and hope in you. We pray that you will help us all to grow closer to you. We pray that you would help those willing to share the message of hope that Jesus brings. We pray that our world, our nations, our churches, and our families might learn to overcome the evil one through Jesus. In his name, Amen.

4/19/95

April 19, 2010

As long as I live, April 19, 1995 will be etched into my memory. It was a beautiful spring morning in Oklahoma City. At 9:02, I was talking on the phone to a dear friend who preaches in Alabama. We were discussing an upcoming seminar when I heard the noise. He also heard it, on the other end of the line in Alabama! "What was that noise?" he asked. I said, "I'm not sure," but it sounded like a swooshing noise, the kind made by an A/C unit turning on in a large building. My secretary knocked on my office door. She came in and told me that there had been some kind of explosion downtown, and that that was all we knew at the time. We turned on a television and immediately began to learn about the horrific explosion at the Murrah Federal Building in the heart of the city.

We hurriedly began making phone calls to check on church members. We had several people who worked in that building from time to time. We learned they were all OK and breathed a small sigh of relief. In a matter of minutes, however, the secretary knocked on the door again and said, "Richard Walton is on the phone for you."

Richard had a difficult time telling me that he believed his wife, Susan, may have been in the building when the bomb exploded. I said, "Stay where you are, I'm on my way."

When I arrived at Richard's office, he informed me that she was on her way to take a college class, but wanted to stop by the federal credit union on her way. She would be there precisely at 9:00 when the credit union opened its doors. We began calling hospitals to see if we could find her but couldn't locate her anywhere. I spent the rest of the day attempting to locate Susan. The good folks at the First Christian Church near the site had made their building available for people to come and learn if their loved ones had survived. As a minister, I was allowed to come and go. I visited with and prayed with a number of families who were waiting there to receive the news. As you can guess, people were shocked and devastated. I spent some time praying and visiting with a grandmother who was waiting to learn about her two precious grandchildren who had been in the child-care facility.

Susan's name was not on either list. I then began to visit some of the hospitals to see if any of them had admitted her. Late that Wednesday afternoon, our shepherds made the wise decision to dismiss our Bible study classes that night and meet together for a special time of prayer. We would pray for Susan and for everyone involved in this terrible tragedy. As we were nearing the end of the service, someone tapped me on the shoulder and said, "Richard Walton is on the phone for you."

Richard told me that Susan had been found, that she was in the hospital, but it didn't look good for her. The elders and I went to the hospital and stayed through the night, praying with and attempting to encourage Richard. The doctors performed three major surgeries that night, and three times they came out to say they didn't think she would make it.

She did make it, and while it took years, she did recover. It took more than thirty surgeries for her to be able to walk again. She started a business to provide women with clothing that is appropriate for work. She has helped hundreds of women. Oh, and by the way, they were able to locate her husband because she gave his phone number in sign language! She was on her way to a sign language class that morning to learn to assist the deaf and hearing impaired.

During the next few days, our lives were a whirlwind. One of the major television stations from Shreveport, LA asked to do a day-long interview. They followed us around everywhere that day. We got as close to the bombing site as anyone was allowed to get. We visited survivors in the hospital and prayed with them. We visited and prayed with families who had lost loved ones. They ran a segment of the story every night on their network news. A part of the feed was picked up by CNN. They attended and recorded our worship service on the following Sunday morning. That day, we discussed the comfort God gives those who are hurting and the fact that God is still in control of our world. A call came from a reporter for the *Chicago Tribune* to see if they could attend our worship service. They interviewed us for the paper. There were numerous other interviews.

After fifteen years, the memories are still vivid. The lessons learned from the tragic event will be with me the rest of my life. I would like to share just a few of the lessons that stand out in my mind.

Sin will cause men to perform unspeakable acts. The damage done on that infamous day was horrific. Nearly 700 people were injured. Of the 188 people who lost their lives that day, 19 of them were children under the age of 6. They were innocent children who had never harmed anyone. Their lives were cut short, not because of some illness, but because of hatred in someone's heart. The blast destroyed or damaged more than 300 buildings in the downtown area. The bomb was estimated to have cost nearly $700 million.

The human spirit is resilient. I had the opportunity to speak with and pray with hundreds of people who were grieving, confused, and questioning what had happened to them. They spoke of their love for the ones who they had lost. They cried tears of pain. They talked of how they would carry the memory of their loved ones with them as long as they lived. They showed great fortitude in the midst of trial. We watched a city, state, and nation come together to rebuild broken lives and shattered hearts.

God's people are compassionate, loving, helpful, and giving. On occasion, I hear some misguided preachers among us speak of how members of the church of Christ are unloving, unkind, etc. Every time I read it in some blog or hear it in a sermon or conversation, I think about what I witnessed in 1995. Literally, millions of dollars poured in from Christians and churches around the world to give to families who needed financial support. Susan Walton received calls, cards, and expressions of support from members of God's family from around the world. I received more calls from preachers, elders, and churches than I can count, asking how they might help. It is my belief that God's people are some of the finest people in the world, and I resent it greatly when I hear some preacher who is critical of the church without really knowing what they are talking about. I watched the members of our congregation rally to support Richard, Susan, and others in more ways than I can describe.

A final lesson from Susan: During the intervening months, Susan probably was interviewed hundreds of times. She would often call me and ask if I would sit in on an interview with her. I sat many times and listened to her tell her story. She never spoke with anger, bitterness, or resentment—but love. When she and Richard were asked to go to Denver for part of the trial, their house burned while they were gone. At first, it was thought foul play was involved, but it was determined that the problem was electrical. Richard and Susan never showed any anger toward God. They never blamed God for their trials.

In one particular interview I was privileged to be in, a reporter said, "Mrs. Walton, how can you not have anger or hatred for those who did this to you?" Her response was classic. It rings in my ears regularly, and I will never forget her wonderful statement. She said, "The Good Book says you can't go to heaven with hate in your heart."

Thank you Susan, for the lessons you taught us during a time of great tragedy in your life.

If you are not from Oklahoma, but you ever get a chance to go, do everything possible to go downtown to the Memorial. It is a beautiful, moving experience. It will help you have a greater understanding of what happened on April 15, 1995. While I still have sorrow in my heart for those who have suffered so much, I thank God for the lessons I learned during those days. Through those lessons, I have been able to better minister to people who are hurting.

A sign at the Memorial says it best with only two words, "WE REMEMBER."

Dear Father, please be with families today who are still grieving the loss of their loved ones because of this terrible tragedy that occurred fifteen years ago today. Bless those who continue to suffer physical and emotional scars because of the sin of others. Dear God, help us to look for people around us who need encouragement. Thank you, Lord, for the many who help during difficult times, those who show your love to the hurting, who do everything possible to make life better for the brokenhearted. Father, help us to encourage one another today. In Jesus' name, Amen.

AN OFFICIAL
AMBASSADOR

June 1, 2010

I t is a privilege for me to serve on a number of boards and advisory councils. All of them have blessed my life in ways that are far beyond what I could have ever imagined. Each one has varying guidelines and goals. They all have specific purposes and plans. One of my friends often reminds those of us who serve as trustees for Freed-Hardeman University that we should always be looking out for funds, friends, and freshmen!

However, I am now an official ambassador and have the document to prove it. Here is how it happened. A few weeks ago, an email arrived inviting me to be a special guest at our local Chick-fil-A to receive a sneak preview of the new Chick-fil-A Spicy Chicken Sandwich. I thought it was awfully nice of them to invite me when there are nearly one hundred thousand people in Lewisville! I accepted their invitation and went by with my "special invitation" printed out to receive my free sandwich. I was welcomed warmly and seated at a special table. The kind lady informed me that because I was their "special guest" today, I would receive not just a sandwich, but also fries and a drink (sweet tea, of course)!

After the meal, the manager came over and asked if I would become an "Official Spicy Chicken Sandwich Ambassador?" I said I would be glad to do so. He said, "You will need to sign this "Official Agreement." What a tremendous idea! As if Chick-fil-A needed more and better marketing! Like many of you, it is one of my favorite places to dine, even before I became one of their Ambassadors. They also happen to have some of the best sweet tea in the world, which moves it up another notch as a dining establishment! Therefore, I am honored to serve as an Ambassador for Chick-fil-A.

What if the church started recruiting members to be ambassadors? It is, after all, a biblical word long before Chick-fil-A or anyone else borrowed it. It is found in 2 Cor. 5:20 where Paul says, "Therefore, we are ambassadors for Christ, God making his appeal through us. We implore you on behalf of Christ, be reconciled to God."

Some have said we can't be ambassadors today in the church the way first century disciples were. The word Paul uses here literally means "to be or to act as an ambassador." It doesn't seem to me that in Scripture this is confined only to people who have seen Christ as some say. However, if you feel strongly about that, at least allow me the opportunity to say that we can be ambassadors in the way our language defines the word. And while it is true we have not seen Christ face-to-face, we have certainly seen him in the lives of others, as well as in Scripture. The image of Christ is to shine in the lives of those who follow him (2 Cor. 4:6).

Chick-fil-A has a great product, but ours is even greater. They have something that will satisfy the body for a short time; we have something that will satisfy the soul forever! Chick-fil-A has some wonderful people who are a part of their organization; my experience has been that the greatest people in the world are a part of the church. Chick-fil-A provides a great atmosphere for families. The church ought to be the greatest place on earth for families! And don't forget, Chick-fil-A is closed on Sunday; we are open every Sunday, and should be every day of the week!

Would you agree to being an ambassador? Would you commit

to telling others the Good News? Will you invite others to be your special guest? Will you tell others about God's free gift to the world? While you may not receive an official certificate, you will receive a reward that is better, an eternal reward.

On second thought, we already are ambassadors. We signed the official agreement the day we gave our life to Jesus. It is a covenant sealed with his blood that we contacted when we were baptized into him for the forgiveness of our sins. He will never let his end of the agreement lapse.

Will we?

Dear Father, help us as your ambassadors to tell everyone we can about the Good News. Help us not to be ashamed or afraid. Help us, dear God, to remember what a tremendous blessing we can be to our friends and family. Please help us to bring as many people as possible to Christ, the One who gives everlasting life. In his name, Amen.

IS THERE A DOCTOR ON BOARD?

June 4, 2010

As I type this, I am 30,000 feet in the air somewhere between Dallas and Birmingham. My schedule tells me that I speak tomorrow morning in Atlanta, and then fly home tomorrow night in time to teach and preach at Lewisville on Sunday.

Prior to our leaving DFW, one of the flight attendants asked over the loud speaker, "Is there a doctor on board? " Apparently, a gentleman in first class was having blood pressure problems. A doctor came forward, checked the man out, and in a few minutes, he was helped off the plane. I'm glad they were able to help him before our departure! Isn't it wonderful to have doctors around at times like these? I thank God for the medical people I know who are always helping others. I said a silent prayer that the man would be okay, and then I started thinking about all the people I know who are hurting.

There are people who have lost loved ones who are grieving because of their loss. There are husbands and wives who are constantly fighting and just can't seem to work out their difficulties. There are couples that are separated or divorced because one of them decided they needed someone different, or they decided it's not worth what it takes to salvage the marriage. There are children who don't understand what is going on with their parents, but they know that something isn't right. Is there a doctor on board?

There are parents who are having massive struggles with teenagers who have made the wrong choices, who are in a relationship with the wrong person, or who are hanging out with the wrong crowd. There are teenagers who are crying out for help from their parents, but the parents are too busy with work or other "important" matters. Is there a doctor on board?

There are parents who have broken hearts because their grown children have walked away from the Lord and his church. They did everything they possibly could to teach their children about the Lord with their lives and their lips, but through other influences, the children chose to walk away. They are concerned about the choices their children are making. Is there a doctor on board?

There are parents who have sent their children off to war. There are husbands/wives who have watched their mates go to war, as well as children who have watched as their dad/mom leave to defend our freedoms in war. They pray daily that their loved ones will come home. Is there a doctor on board?

There are homeless, hungry, and hurting people on our streets, wondering if anyone will see them, wondering where they will get their next meal and where they will sleep tonight. Is there a doctor on board?

There are people who fear that their chance in life will be hijacked. They have been ridiculed, ostracized, and alienated because of the color of their skin or their nationality. There are people who fear that their country will be hijacked. They have been marginalized and unappreciated because of their values and beliefs. Is there a doctor on board?

There are people who sit in church buildings filled to capacity every Sunday who feel like they are all alone in the world. There are teens that come to church, but they don't feel that they have any friends. There are people who attend worship with broken hearts because of disappointment in their home, at work, or in their walk with God. Is there a doctor on board?

There are the preachers who preach their hearts out and wonder if anyone is listening, who work their heads off and wonder if anyone recognizes it. There are preachers who study diligently for hours and hours, and then someone is critical because of a missed Scripture reference or a mispronounced word. There are preachers who wonder from week to week if they will have a job. There are preachers who love the church where they work, but they feel compelled to leave because they don't want their children to see the fighting. Is there a doctor on board?

There are shepherds who meet for hours each week, spending time in prayer for those they serve, but no one says thank you. There are elders who freely give of their time to visit, to counsel families, to discuss ministries, and to mediate disagreements, and then they receive ridicule because someone doesn't like a minor decision they have made. Is there a doctor on board?

There are missionaries who have given their lives in God's service, who live thousands of miles from their family and friends, who are worried they might lose their support. Is there a doctor on board?

There are older church members who are in deep pain because they have given their lives, time, prayers, money, and everything else they have to help the church, and then some young leaders decide that everything has to change with no regard for the past. Is there a doctor on board?

There are young people who are hurting because they feel as though they are in dying churches where you can't sing new songs, can't change the order of worship, and can't ask questions for fear that you will be "set straight." Is there a doctor on board?

There are Christians who are dealing with all kinds of sins and they are wondering if there is any hope, any help, any one who cares? Is there a doctor on board?

The good news for all of us is that there is a doctor on board. He is Jesus, the Great Physician. A long time ago, he and his Father put two pieces of wood together and opened a doctor's office that can heal every wounded heart, every scarred life, every broken relationship and every hurting soul that exists in our world. Jesus, our Savior, came into this world to heal people. He came into the world to show us a better way to live. He came to bring peace to our homes, our churches, and to everyone in the world. He came into the world so that homes can be better and happier. He came to bring us an abundant life. But he came primarily to help us escape the clutches of sin and Satan. He came to save us, to set us free from sin, to give us eternal life.

The Great Physician wants to come on board in your life; he stands at the door of your heart and knocks to gain entrance. Will you let him in? Will you let him take away your hurt, your pain, and your sorrow? Will you let the Great Physician on board to help?

Dear Father, thank you for sending Jesus, the Great Physician, into our world. Thank you for making it possible for us to be healed, made whole, and forgiven. Dear God, help us to let Jesus on board in our life so that we can be all that you desire us to be. Father, help those who are hurting to turn to the one who can make all things good. In Jesus' name, Amen.

HEALTHY
FAMILIES

We live in a culture obsessed with health. There are health food stores, heart-healthy choices in restaurants, health diets, health clubs, special healthy foods for pets, and you can even buy special health food for your plants. We definitely live in a "health conscience" society. It seems that we think about health in every facet of our life, except the one that is most important. Is it possible that we have become so fascinated with becoming healthy that we have forgotten about having a healthy family? Amazon.com offers 39,077 books on Health: Mind and Body and only 6,678 on Parenting and Families. While the family is not finished, it appears to be very fragile in today's society.

Healthy families don't just happen. Just as with developing and maintaining a healthy mind and body, it will require a great deal of time and effort on our part to develop and maintain a healthy family. Healthy families are the result of wise decisions and wise actions. A long time ago, King Solomon said, "By wisdom a house is built, and by understanding it is established" (Prov. 24:3). One translation says, "It takes wisdom to have a good family, and it takes understanding to make it strong" (NCV).

If we are going to make wise decisions and take wise action, we must ask God to help us. We must also return to the Word of God to help us know how to have a healthy family. We will not have perfect families, because families are composed of people, and there are no perfect people. But with God's help, we can have families that are pleasing to him. Let's consider some observations from the Word of God that will help create healthy families.

We should prepare our children for life. One of the great goals for all parents is to provide our children with all the necessary tools they need for life, and it must begin early. It is during the early years of a child's life that the most basic and important life skills are learned: walking, eating and language development. It is also during these early years that children begin to develop important skills such as how to relate to others, how to build character in their lives, and which values are most important. In other words, they learn the foundation upon which they will later build their spiritual life. Parents must never forget the critical role they play in the development of their children during these early years.

In Luke 2:52, it is said that Jesus grew "in wisdom and in stature and in favor with God and man." This is a marvelous example of the four primary areas of growth. Wisdom indicates intellectual or mental growth, stature indicates physical growth, in favor with man indicates social growth, and in favor with God represents the most important growth which is spiritual growth. These should be the goals that we have for each of our children. If we can encourage this growth in our children, it will ensure healthy families for generations to come.

In Deut. 6:1-5, we read God's charge to his people as they prepare to enter the Land of Promise. In verses 6-7 of this great chapter we read, "These words that I command you today shall be on your heart. You shall teach them diligently to your children, and shall talk of them when you sit in your house, and when you walk by the way, and when you lie down, and when you rise."

The Bible is clear that the responsibility to rear children is placed squarely at the feet of the parents. Today, too many parents want to relinquish the responsibility of rearing their children to others, but God says, you (parents), not the government, not the school system, and not even the church is responsible. He says, "you shall, or you must," which indicates this is not an option. Not if you choose to do this, or if you have time to do this, but you must do this!

He says, you must "teach." We are always teaching our children by what we do and what we say. All parents, especially those with small children, need to remember that children are like sponges, soaking up every word they hear. God says, you must teach my commandments. These are God's demands for our lives, and he attaches a promise to this injunction. If you do this, it will be well with you and your children (Deut. 6:1–2).

We should guard our children from the storms of life. Every parent has approached the throne of God and begged him to protect their children from harm. We have prayed for their safety when they are away from us. We have prayed that they would be protected from disease, sickness, and death. This is as it should be. However, parents must also remember that physical storms are only one type of storm that should concern us. There are also the mental and emotional storms that our children will face. We want our children to study hard and learn all they can about life so that they can be guarded from the emotional and mental storms of life.

Another category of critical storms that should cause great concern to Christian parents are the spiritual storms of life. The Bible teaches that each individual is in a daily battle with Satan, and that we must be aware of his schemes or devices (Eph. 6:10–17). In our postmodern culture, our children are being told that there is no such thing as absolute truth, and that what one believes is of little importance. In this culture war, we must never forget that Jesus said, "You will know the truth, and the truth will set you free" (John 8:32).

In addition to the storms that rage in the larger religious culture, perhaps the most dangerous to our children are the storms raging in the church. There was a day when families could walk into just about any congregation of God's people and know what was going to be taught. There was a day when parents could send their children to any Christian university and know that they would be taught the same biblical doctrines that have always been taught in the church. However, those statements are no longer true. This places an even greater responsibility on parents to assure that their children have the spiritual knowledge and skills needed to be discerning in what they hear in congregations and in universities (Heb. 5:12–14).

We should guide our children to the Lord. As previously stated, it is during the early years of a child's life that they are most impressionable. Occasionally, I will hear some parent say, "We don't want to impose our values on our children; we want them to make their own choices." We do not use that kind of faulty logic in any other area of our children's lives. We do not allow them to choose if they will go to school, what time they will go to bed, or what they will eat. We make those important life-decisions for them while they are young. The fact is that our children are going to learn and develop their values and their beliefs about the Lord from someone. One way to look at our responsibility is that we are to take our children from parent-control, to self-control, to God-control.

The people of God in Moses' day were told that they should remind their children how God had delivered them from Egyptian captivity (Deut. 6:20–25). Likewise, we must remind our children that the Lord rescued us from sin and Satan. There are a number of ways that we can guide our children to the Lord.

First, we can guide our children to the Lord through the lessons that are learned. Moses said that the statutes of God must be taught. He commanded the parents, "You shall teach them diligently to your children, and shall talk of them when you sit in your house, and when you walk by the way, and when you lie down, and when you rise" (Deut. 6:7). Submitting to this passage means it will take a great effort and much time on our part.

Second, we can guide our children to the Lord through the life we live. Our children learn not only by what they hear, but also by what they see. If we say one thing and do something different, our children will pick up on it. If we tell them to put the Lord first, and we don't put the Lord first, they will see our inconsistencies. If we tell them to be honest, and we are not honest, they will know. There is an old adage that says, "I cannot hear what you are saying, because what you are keeps ringing in my ears."

A third way we can guide our children to the Lord is through the legacy we leave. We may leave our children a nice home or a large inheritance, but the greatest gift we can leave our children is the remembrance of a happy, healthy, Christian home. The happy memories of a Christian home are greater than any earthly, physical gift we can give to our families.

Dear Father, we pray for families who are struggling today. We pray that all of us will recognize how much we need you at the center of our family. May each of us grow closer to you and to one another. Help us to follow your plan as we seek to grow stronger in our families. In Jesus' name, Amen.

HOW DO YOU
TREAT THIS BOOK?

May 22, 2012

I t must be a very important document. The rules associated with it
show that it is loved and respected.

- One should make formal ablutions before handling
  this book or reading from its text.

- One who is in need of a formal bath should not touch
  this book until after bathing.

- A non-member should not handle the sacred text,
  but may listen to tapes of it or handle a translation or
  exegesis.

- Those who are unable to handle this book based on
  these reasons should either avoid handling it completely,
  or in necessity hold it while using some sort of barrier
  covering the hand, such as a cloth or a glove.

- In addition, when one is not reading or reciting from
  this book, it should be closed and stored in a clean,
  respectable place. Nothing should be placed on top
  of it, nor should it ever be placed on the floor or in a
  bathroom.

- To further show respect for the sacred text, those who

are writing it should use clear, elegant handwriting, and those who are reading from it should use clear, beautiful voices.

Some of you may be thinking that these rules surely concern the Bible. Oh, how we could wish! According to Islam, this is how a follower is to treat the Koran. Compare those rules to the way that some people treat their Bibles.

1. Leave it at the church building and never open it, except when you come to Bible class or worship.

2. Leave it in the car where it can become discolored by the sun and where it can be stepped on, sat on, or otherwise treated poorly.

3. Throw it around as if it is just any book and treat it like it is just another book in the library.

I know that not everybody treats their Bible like this, but I'm afraid that many do. So how should we treat the Bible? Do we have to be gentle? Do we have to treat it with kid gloves? Do we need to bathe or wash our hands before we read the Bible?

A recent research project by the Barna Group revealed the following facts about what Americans think about the Bible.

- 85% of households own at least one Bible, with a household average of 4.3 Bibles.

- 69% of Americans believe the Bible provides answers on how to live a meaningful life.

- 36% of Americans read the Bible less than once a year.

- 79% of those surveyed believe they are knowledgeable about the Bible, but 54% were unable to identify the first five books of the Bible.

- 46% believe the Bible, the Koran, and the Book of
  Mormon are different expressions of the same spiritual
  truths.

Allow me to share a few thoughts in response.

Treat the Bible like it is God's inspired Word. "All Scripture is breathed out by God and profitable for teaching, for reproof, for correction, and for training in righteousness" (2 Tim. 3:16). This is how God has chosen to communicate his Word, his will, and his way to us. It is a history book, but it is so much more. It is a book filled with science, but it is so much more. It is a book that teaches us about finances, but it is so much more. It is a book that teaches us about marriage, the family, and how to raise children, but it is so much more. It is a book that teaches us about church organization, but it is so much more. It is a book about relationships, but it is so much more. It is the inspired, inerrant, irrefutable, Word of our loving Father.

Treat the Bible like it is your guide for this life. The Psalmist said, "Your word is a lamp to my feet and a light to my path" (Psa. 119:105). The Bible is like a road map. If you are lost, it will help you find your way. If you are in darkness, it will lead you to light. If you are alone, it will serve as your companion. If you are out of spiritual energy, it will fill your tank. If you are meeting road blocks, it will redirect you to better roads. If you are struggling with storms, it will help protect you.

Treat the Bible like you love it. Consider again the words of the Psalmist: "Oh how I love your law! It is my meditation all the day" (Psa. 119:97). I have a wonderful library of books. Some of them I purchased, but many of them were passed down to me by my father. Some were given to me as gifts. They are all precious to me. Some are more precious than others. There are some that I will loan to anyone that can use them to help in their study. There are others that I am more careful about loaning out. In fact, if I let you touch some of these treasures, you had better not harm them in any way! Don't get me wrong—I'm not saying that we should ever refuse anyone the right to read the Bible. I only wonder what would happen if we viewed the Bible as a priceless treasure!

Treat the Bible like it is the only book that can get you to heaven. There are millions of self-help books available. There are many books to help you diet and exercise. There are many books to help you with home repairs or fix a broken-down car. There are many books to help you learn about history or the arts. There are many books to help you with relationships, parenting, or marriage. But there is only one book to help you get to heaven. "Receive with meekness the implanted word, which is able to save your souls" (Jas. 1:21).

Treat the Bible as if your eternal life depends on it. Jesus said, "The one who rejects me and does not receive my words has a judge; the word that I have spoken will judge him on the last day" (John 12:48). In Rev. 20:12, John gives us a glimpse of what it will be like on the great Day of Judgment. "And I saw the dead, great and small, standing before the throne, and books were opened. Then another book was opened, which is the book of life. And the dead were judged by what was written in the books, according to what they had done." Someday, we will all stand before the judgment throne of God. When we do, we will be judged on how we lived in view of what the Bible teaches.

How do you feel about your Bible?

Dear Father, help us realize how important your Word is to our lives here on this earth, as well as our eternal destination. Help us to treat your Word with as much love and respect as we can find in our hearts. Help us, dear Lord, to obey your Word and help us to use it as the basis of every decision in our life. In Jesus' name, Amen.

FROM DEATH
TO LIFE

February 27, 2012

Melissa has worked in a cancer center for more than twenty years. She has always been a kind, thoughtful person. Her smile is infectious. She causes every patient who comes under her care to feel better about their struggles. It would be impossible to count the number of people who lost their battle with cancer who have been lovingly cared for by Melissa.

We have some ladies in our congregation who volunteer at the cancer center and have had the privilege of working closely with Melissa. She has cared for numerous other members of the Lewisville church. She cared for a number of our members who have passed from this life to the next. All of our members who have been under Melissa's care have been wonderful examples to her.

Some time ago, at the invitation of some of our members, she started visiting our worship assemblies on Sunday morning. Someone asked her if she would study the Bible with her. Her response was that she didn't want to be rushed or pressured.

A few weeks ago, one of our members just handed her a copy of a simple self-study guide that was written by another of our wonderful ladies. Melissa started studying; about a week later, she told the sister who had given her the study guide that she was ready to be baptized.

This wonderful lady, one who has been such a great comfort to those passing from this life to the next, is now our sister. The one who has assisted others in passing from physical life to physical death has now passed from spiritual death to spiritual life.

We praise God for her decision and for her new life. I am convinced that the children of God who have come under her care have helped her, just as she has helped them. There are several lessons we as Christians can learn from this wonderful event.

It is important to build relationships with the people in our lives. Building relationships is not easy. The people we work with, go to school with, and live in neighborhoods with are all just as busy as we are. It takes a great deal of time and effort in our fast-paced world to get to know people. We need to work to learn names, to learn about family situations, to get to know the people in our lives. Building friendships is one of the very best ways to reach people with the glorious gospel of Jesus.

Invite those we know to join us when we worship. At first, it may seem odd and strange to invite people we don't know well to worship with us. However, the more we do that, the easier it will become. When we are kind to the people we meet, it will be easier to invite them to worship with us. A simple invitation may be the beginning of leading someone to Jesus. Don't quit the first time you are told no. Keep inviting.

Talk about Jesus and his church in positive ways. In our conversations, we need to let people know we are Christians. We can talk about some event or activity that is happening in our home congregation. We can talk about our church friends, about what we are studying in Bible class, or about a current sermon series. We should always speak in such a way that people around us will know we are Christians. The apostle Paul said, "Let your speech always be gracious, seasoned with salt" (Col. 4:6). Paul also told us that we should only speak words that are edifying (Eph. 4:29).

Live every day in a way that honors and glorifies God. Paul admonishes us with these words, "Whatever you do, in word or deed, do everything in the name of the Lord Jesus, giving thanks to God the Father through him" (Col. 3:17). It is easier to live a committed Christian life when everything seems to be going right in life, but the real test of our honoring God is when life comes undone. When we lose someone dear to us, when we learn we have contacted cancer, when we have lost our job, when our children are not living as they should, when we are struggling in our marriage, when we are going through other difficulties—do we live lives that glorify God during these times?

People are watching us to see how we live. They want to know how we handle adversity and how we deal with life. Paul said that our lives are like a letter, written on the hearts of others (2 Cor. 3:2). There are so many people just like Melissa who need to learn how to pass from death to life. We have opportunities every day to show people in our life how they can become children of God. By the way, Melissa has handed that study guide to her husband!

Who will we influence today?

Who can we invite to worship?

Who will we attempt to reach for Jesus today?

Dear Father, help us to realize how important it is for us to live for you every day. Help us to be aware of the people around us. Help us, dear God, to face adversity with grace and commitment. Help us to tell others about Jesus and his church. Help us to invite our friends, family, co-workers, and neighbors to worship with us. Help us to understand that we can help lead others from death to life. Thank you, Father, for all that you do for us every day. In Jesus' name, Amen.

LESSONS
FROM DAD

June 14, 2010

This Sunday is Father's Day. There will be thousands of Father's Day messages preached all across America. My plan for Sunday is to take a different approach to the Father's Day message than I have in the past.

A dear friend told me recently that it seemed every Mother's Day the message was about how wonderful our mothers are, and how we should all learn to treat them better. Then came the stinger. He said Father's Day messages (including mine) are typically about how fathers need to be better fathers, and about how they should improve their lives. The more I think about it, the more I believe he is right. I feel I owe an apology to the fathers who have heard me preach on Father's Day.

It is not popular being a father in our time. Fathers seem to always get a bad rap, even in many pulpits across the country. Have you noticed how dads on TV are often portrayed as being pitiful, inept, and sorry? Even professional athletes say hi to "mom," yet hardly ever speak to dad! I am not saying that moms should not receive this praise and adoration, only that there are many dads in the world who should receive more praise than they get.

So this Sunday, my message will be entitled, "Lessons From Dad."

With a heart filled with gratitude to good dads, here is a sampling of the lessons my dad taught me.

The Bible is the Word of God; therefore, we should obey it. My dad believed (and still does) that the Bible is the inspired, inerrant, perfect, and complete Word of God. He taught us to love God's Word. I vividly recall how his sermons were always engulfed in the Word. He quoted a lot of passages, but he always made application of the Scripture to our lives. He taught us that we would be judged ultimately by Scripture (John 12:48); therefore, we should obey all of God's Word. I remember growing up thinking that dad didn't just know the Bible; it was the basis of how he lived his life.

We should always put the Lord first. There were never any questions in our home about who was first in our lives. The words of our Savior recorded in Matt. 6:33 were the basis for everything we did. There were three boys and one girl in our home. We all loved sports, and we played every sport you could play. But we learned quickly that the Lord and his church would always come before our sporting events. Many times, we would come to Bible study on Wednesday night dressed in our team uniform because we had been pulled out of a game to make it in time, or we would leave Bible study and get to a game late. Our worship to God and our Bible study always received priority over our school studies. The work of the Lord was always put before any school or secular activities.

Every person is special and deserves to be loved because they are created in God's image. Our dad taught us the importance and value of every person. I can vividly recall dad taking time to speak with or visit with people that did not seem to matter to others. He would visit in the home of people who were destitute. He would help people who were suffering and going through difficult times. He would speak in a kind way to anyone, anywhere. Dad taught us that the color of a person's skin, their standing in the community, their ability to give to the church, their educational degrees, or their business clout did not matter. What mattered most was that they were created in God's image; therefore, they were important.

Every individual has a soul that will last forever; therefore, we should help them prepare for eternity. Perhaps more than anything else, dad taught us the value of each individual's soul. He would talk to anyone about Jesus. He taught us that everyone is a sinner (Rom. 3:23), and that everyone will stand before God in judgment (Heb. 9:27). He taught us that everyone needs Jesus. I can remember going with dad into homes that had only a dirt floor to show them the old Jule Miller filmstrips (the set with the old record player that dinged to let you know it was time to manually move to the next frame!). Dad's greatest attribute has always been his desire to help others find their way to heaven.

The value of hard work. My dad learned the value of working hard from his father. Dad tells the story about a time when someone came to our home when I was a small boy and knocked on our door. This sales person asked me if my dad was at work. I responded by saying, "My dad doesn't work; he is a preacher!" As I grew older and watched dad, I learned just how untrue that was. In addition, I have learned it in my own life. Dad believed working hard was something that every Christian should do.

The importance of respecting your elders. My thought here is primarily about the leaders in the church, but includes everyone who is older. I never once heard my dad say one unkind word about a shepherd in the church. Come to think about it, I never heard him speak an unkind word about anyone. Dad believed he worked under the authority of God's shepherds, and he has always had a great deal of respect for them. Many times in recent years, I have been thankful for the times dad allowed us to be associated with older preachers, as well as other older Christians whose lives were filled with wisdom that could help us along the way. The wise man said a long time ago, "Gray hair is a crown of glory; it is gained in a righteous life" (Prov. 16:31).

Dad, I haven't said it enough through the years, but allow me to say it now. Thank you for the valuable life lessons you have taught me, and continue to teach me even now. Thank you most of all for teaching me to show the love of Jesus to others. I am eternally thankful to you, and I love you dearly.

Dear Father, thank you for strong, godly fathers. Thank you for the lessons they teach us on a regular basis. Thank you for allowing us to be instructed by men who love you and who have a strong desire to help us be like you. Thank you, dear God, for men who allow the light of Jesus to shine through them. Help us to emulate the qualities that are a part of their lives. Help us to draw on their experience and their wisdom. Thank you, for being the perfect Father, the one who loves us most! Thank you for all that you continually do to help us be closer to you. In Jesus' name, Amen.

MAKING HIS
PARENTS PROUD

October 2, 2010

This morning, I boarded an early flight to make the trip from Dallas to Birmingham. I left my new granddaughter and my family in Oklahoma to come to Birmingham to be with my dad. A few weeks ago, dad suffered some mini-strokes. None of them were debilitating or caused long-term damage. He had some numbness in his left hand, but the doctor said it would go away with therapy.

He seemed to be doing better, and in fact on Thursday had been moved to a rehab facility. Yesterday, Dad had another stroke. This one was more serious. It has affected his ability to communicate. It is too early to tell how long his speech will be affected. I am not sure how much dad is able to recognize those of us who are around him. We believe he can, and that he can hear us, but he just can't communicate to us yet.

One thing I do know—it is not easy to see a man in this condition who has so boldly proclaimed the Good News to so many around the world. The number of people who have heard our dad proclaim the gospel is mind-boggling. It is also very strange for him to be in a hospital room, being visited and cared for by others. When I was a boy, and even during my teenage years, I made numerous hospital visits with my dad to encourage those who were hurting. He is the consummate minister, and he attempted to pass that along to his children.

I got on the plane this morning in Dallas, and a man walked out of the cockpit in a pilot's suit and grabbed the mike from the flight attendant. He said, "Ladies and gentlemen, this is a very special day. Everyone will be extra safe today, because for the first time in my life, I am flying my parents to their destination!" Everyone on the plane applauded. I thought to myself, "His parents must be really, really proud of him!" All during the flight, I prayed a lot, and I thought a lot about how we should all do our very best to make our parents proud.

We can make our parents proud by remembering what they taught us. Solomon was one of the wisest men who ever lived. He had a lot to say to children about how they should remember what they learned from their parents, and how they should not forsake the teaching of their parents. I would encourage you to go back and read Prov. 1:8–10; 2:1–5; 3:1–4; 4:1–6; 5:1–2; 7:1–2.

We can make our parents proud by taking care of them when they need us. We must never forget how our parents provided for us, cared for us, nurtured us, and taught us when we could not do any of that for ourselves. The apostle Paul said that anyone who would not provide for their own families is worse than an unbeliever (1 Tim. 5:8). This would include our providing and caring for our parents when they need us most.

We can make our parents proud by showing love to other members of our families. There are times when families become estranged, and there is not much communication. How wonderful when family unity can be restored and broken bridges can be mended. When the Bible tells us that we are to live at peace with all men (Rom. 12:18; Heb. 12:14), that would definitely include our family.

We can make our parents proud by continuing the legacy they pass down to us. All of us receive a legacy from our families, and we do well when we pass down to our children and grandchildren what we receive from our parents. May God help us to pass on the teachings of God to future generations.

We can make our parents proud when we make our heavenly Father proud. God is the ultimate example for all parents, and when our parents have attempted to please him, we should follow their lead.

Dear Father, we thank you for giving us our parents. We give you thanks for the legacy they have passed down to us. Help us, dear Lord, to remember what they have taught us, help us to care for our parents when they need us, help us to love our family more, and help us, Father, to honor our parents by honoring you. In Jesus' name, Amen.

FAMILY &
FRIENDS

October 6, 2010

Tonight, I'm spending another restless night with my Dad in his hospital room. This is my second night to stay with him, just the two of us. It has been my privilege to be with him since last Saturday, except for a few hours. I have talked to him, quoted Scripture to him, sung to him, and prayed with him. The only problem is he can't communicate with me. Oh, how I wish I could hear his strong voice talk about kindness, winning souls, how we need to love the Lord, and a thousand other topics as I have done so many times in the past.

The first night, I slept about an hour. I am hoping I will get a little more this time. We are about to be in day five since Dad had a pretty serious stroke. Our outstanding doctor has said that we are in the most crucial days of the post-stroke period.

Dad is still not responding, but the doctor says that's not uncommon. He hopes dad will respond after day five or six. We are praying he will begin to respond and will regain his wonderful ability to communicate.

During this past week I've been reminded of the importance of family and friends. There are times in our lives when we are reminded of the importance of the people closest to us. During the past week, family and friends from around the world have blessed us.

I have watched our family come together to surround our dad with love and attention. I have watched family members put aside differences to work together to show the common love we have for dad.

I have had friends drive for hours to come to the hospital, knowing they would not be allowed into the room, just to spend a few minutes visiting and praying with us. Some of these friends have been a part of my life for more than thirty years. The blessing they continue to be to our life is overwhelming.

Here are a few valuable lessons that I have been reminded of by family and friends this week.

Tell people you love them. The number of times this week that I have heard the words, "I love your Dad," "I love you," or "we love your family" has been overwhelming. We all know that God's Word teaches we should love one another (John 13:34–35; 1 John 2:9–10; 3:14–18), but hearing someone say those three magic words makes a tremendous difference.

Show people you love them. If saying the words is important, showing love by our actions carries love to the next step. Jesus said, "If you love me, you will keep my commandments" (John 14:15). This is love by action. If we really love someone, we will show them we love them. My family has seen love in action during this struggle. People have brought food, sent cards, offered their homes for out-of-town guests, driven for hours to sit for a visit, and shown kindness in numerous other ways.

Pray for those you love. Prayer is one of the most powerful resources Christians have at our disposal. We can approach the throne of God with boldness and know he hears us (Heb. 4:14–16). We have the assurance that Jesus our Savior mediates for us when we pray (1 Tim. 2:5). Even when we are at a loss for words (as I have been some in recent days), and when we can only utter, "God help us," the loving Spirit intercedes for us (Rom. 8:26–27). We have heard from people throughout the world who let us know they are praying for us. To each one who has come by and prayed for us, to each church who has offered up special prayers for us, to every individual who has told us that we are in your prayers, thank you is insufficient. We feel we have been bathed and overwhelmed by the prayers of righteous people! There are not enough words in our vocabulary to properly say thank you.

It is not my intention to make this about just my family, but this is my perspective at this time. I am well aware of the fact that there are thousands of other Christians around the world who are going through similar challenges right now. There are Christians being physically persecuted, Christians who have lost someone close to them, Christians who have lost their jobs with no assurance of future work, Christians who are dealing with death, disease, depression, and dejection. There are Christians who are dealing with division in their church. There are Christians struggling with some private sin, those who are questioning their faith, and they are desperately trying to find their way back to God. There are Christians who are going through marriage problems, dealing with divorce, and alienation from their children. There are Christians who have left their first love.

We need one another! There are so many shattered hopes, broken homes, and bruised lives in our world. WE DESPERATELY NEED ONE ANOTHER. We have no way of knowing for sure what is going to happen with dad's situation or with any of the situations I've mentioned above. However, we do know that God is on his Throne, that God is good, and that he will ultimately work everything out for our good. With this knowledge in our hearts and heads, and with the help of one another, we can endure any difficulty or hardship that comes our way.

Dear God up in heaven, help us not to just talk about Jesus; help us to become Jesus. Help us, Father, not to just talk about being loving

Christians; help us to say the words, "I love you." Help us to show our love by our actions, and help us to pray for one another more. Dear God, teach us to be all that you want us to be and all that those around us need us to be. Thank you, Father, for showing us how we should live. In Jesus' name, Amen.

THROUGH A
CHILD'S EYES

November 4, 2010

Since returning home from dad's funeral last Saturday, much of my time has been spent attempting to express gratitude to the countless people who have shown the Lord's compassion during this extremely difficult time. Shortly after dad's death, I started a mailbox in my email and called it simply, "Notes About Dad." Currently, that mailbox has 681 messages, with more arriving each day. During the past week, I have attempted to answer every one of those messages. Answering these has been good for me. It has caused me to go back and reread what many wrote about dad and our family. Many of them have brought tears of joy and thankfulness to our hearts.

In addition, hundreds of sympathy cards have arrived at our home and at the office from literally all over the world. There have also been phone calls from around the world. For each of these expressions of comfort, we are truly thankful. We do not feel worthy, but we are thankful and humbled by the kindness of so many.

Then there are the children. Words of comfort, pictures, notes and love from the children. I would like to take a few minutes to share with you some thoughts from just a few of the children. To see death and heaven through a child's eyes is enlightening. It is beautiful and encouraging. The theology may not be exactly right every time,

but the thoughts of a child's heart will certainly make us think...
And there are times that the theology of children makes more sense
than some adults'!

After dad passed away, one of our children's Bible classes was
praying for Mr. Jeff and his family. They were also praying for others
who had special concerns. They were talking about ways we could
help others. One of the little girls said, "Who is in Mr. Jeff's corner?"
This little girl had heard her mother talk about how everybody needs
somebody in their "corner" at different times. This sweet little girl
wanted to make sure someone was taking care of everyone. We all
need the Lord, the church, our family, and our friends in our "corner"
at various times in our life.

Last week, I received an e-mail from one of our Christian friends
who related the conversation she had with her two children (ages 6
and 4). Here is part of what she wrote. "This morning, I told them
that your dad had passed, and that you were very sad and would
need a big hug from them when you got back. They both looked at
me kind of funny. One said exactly 'But he's with God now, mom.
We all want to go to heaven.' And then the other, 'And God will heal
him. Now he can play.' If I had any idea of the response, I would have
recorded it for you to hear yourself." How wonderful.

At the close of services on Sunday, a man brought me two
homemade cards. His daughters wanted to make a card that would
help ease the pain. They wanted to draw pictures, and they asked
what would make Mr. Jeff feel better. My friend told them that
knowing my dad was in heaven is the best thing I can know. So they
decided to draw pictures of heaven. One had the gates, the streets of
gold, an angel, and a picture of a zebra. My friend said, "Apparently,
my daughter thinks there should be zebras in heaven!" The other
had a picture of heaven and of her talking with Deborah, the judge in
the Bible. My friend said his daughter was fascinated with Deborah.

Another little boy came running up to me Sunday and wanted

to give me a big hug. He said, "I love you Mr. Jeff, and I thought you would need a big hug!" How right he was.

No wonder Jesus said, "Truly, I say to you, unless you turn and become like children, you will never enter the kingdom of heaven. Whoever humbles himself like this child is the greatest in the kingdom of heaven. Whoever receives one such child in my name receives me" (Matt 18:3–5). "Let the little children come to me and do not hinder them, for to such belongs the kingdom of heaven" (Matt. 19:14).

While we are extremely thankful for every expression of comfort we have received, there is something special about these words from children. May God help us to realize how precious they are, and how important it is for us to continue teaching them the Word of God.

Dear Father, we thank you for the fact that we are blessed to serve the God of all comfort. We thank you for the opportunity to receive your comfort through others. Dear God, we thank you in a special way for children. Through their innocence, they teach us. They help us learn more about the sweetness of heaven and about your love. Help us, Lord, to always give attention to the needs of children, and help us never to quit teaching them your marvelous Word. In Jesus' name, Amen.

GOD IS
SO GOOD

October 17, 2011

The past year has been extremely difficult for me on a number of levels. I have had some challenges in my personal life and in my work that have caused me to spend a lot of extra time in prayer. Even as I have struggled with these issues, I am constantly reminded of the goodness of God.

God is good because of his love. It's amazing to consider how much God loves us, even when we don't deserve it (John 3:16; Rom. 5:8).

God is good because of his gifts. Every physical and spiritual blessing we enjoy is because of God's goodness (Jas. 1:17; Eph. 1:3).

God is good because of his comfort. When we have pain in our hearts, he is still the God of all comfort (2 Cor. 1:3–5).

God is good because of his church. It is in the church that we find encouragement when we are down (Heb. 10:22–25). One of the bright spots in my life through this year has been the blessing of being a part of a wonderful church family. Our friends who are a part of the church can make every burden easier to bear (Gal. 6:1–2).

God is good because of family. It was our Father in heaven who declared, "It is not good for man to be alone" (Gen. 2:18). When God ordained marriage, he knew the importance of a husband and wife leaning on one another through difficult times. The greatest blessing in my life during this past year without a doubt has been the support and encouragement of a loving wife. Praise God for his infinite wisdom in designing marriage. Another great blessing has been the joy of spending time with our precious granddaughter. Surely, God knew that we needed grandchildren as we grow older.

God is good because of friendship. In addition to our friends in the local church, one of the greatest blessings in this life has been preaching friends. We have been encouraged so many times by preachers young and old. It has been encouraging to be associated with older preachers who have many of the same struggles we endure. Listening to these men of God discuss the work of preaching, the church, family, and life has blessed us more than we can explain. It has been equally encouraging to be associated with a younger generation of preachers. These young men are preaching the unsearchable riches of Christ and continuing the work of God; they are a tremendous blessing. Of course, the greatest friend we have is Jesus. He was willing to lay down his life for us (John 15:13). He has promised us that he will always be with us (Matt. 28:20; Heb. 13:5).

God is good because of his promises. Every promise from our Father is great and precious (2 Pet. 1:3–4) His promises are found on every page of Scripture. To see how God fulfilled his promises in the lives of his people throughout time is a great reminder that he keeps all of his promises.

The beloved apostle Paul understood what it is like to endure difficult times in this life. "So we do not lose heart. Though our outer self is wasting away, our inner self is being renewed day by day. For this light momentary affliction is preparing for us an eternal weight of glory beyond all comparison" (2 Cor. 4:16-17). My prayer for all of you is that, as you endure hardships in this life, that these reminders will be of help to you.

Dear Father, we thank you for comforting us when we are weak. We thank you for knowing what we need most, and for giving us what we need most at every turn in our lives. Help us, dear God, to trust you more and to remember how much you love us. Thank you for all you have done and continue to do for us. In Jesus' name, Amen.

SHE CHOSE TO
ATTEND WORSHIP

December 2, 2010

The last sit down face-to-face conversation I had with my dad before he passed away was June 5, 2010. I had been asked to speak for the Georgia School of Preaching Lectureship in Atlanta. I decided to fly into Birmingham, have lunch with dad if he was available, then drive over to Atlanta. We met at Chick-fil-A for lunch. As it turned out, we were able to sit and visit for a couple of hours. It was a memorable visit for a number of reasons.

Looking back on our visit, it seems obvious to me now that dad was not well. He seemed tired and, for the first time in my life, he seemed old. I had no idea that in about four months he would be gone. If I had only known, I would have attempted to visit with him for several more hours. There is so much I want to talk to him about even now.

Dad asked about Laura and the children, we discussed our work with the church, and talked about upcoming speaking engagements. Then I asked dad if we could talk a little about the Jenkins family history. In recent years, I've wanted to learn more about our family heritage; I guess it's an age thing. Particularly, I was interested in hearing about my great-grandmother.

Dad had told me the story about his grandmother before, but I asked him to tell me again to the best of his memory. I will not give you all the details, but here is to the best of my memory what he told me.

Big Mama (the family name for my great-grandmother) was an amazing woman. She had been a Christian, but she married a man who was not a Christian. She went to worship with God's people on a regular basis, but when the children came along, it was more difficult.

Her husband did not want her to go, and he made it extremely hard for her. On one occasion, he rigged the car so it wouldn't start, so she walked to church. She spoke once about a Gospel meeting taking place in the local church and she attended. She heard the preacher talk about the need for faithfulness to God and about faithfulness in attending all the services.

She made up her mind then to attend, no matter what. One night, as she was leaving, her husband was trying to get her not to go. As she was leaving, she heard him whipping the children. The children were crying for her, but she went on. She stated that she did not get much out of the service that night. When she returned home, he had locked the door, and all the lights were out. She didn't know what he might have done to the children. She knocked on the door, but he wouldn't let her in. She hollered in and said, "Arthur, I'm going to get the constable." He finally let her in.

The next morning, she went out to the field where he was working. She said, "Arthur, I don't know what you are going to do to me, but I want you to know, I've made up my mind and nothing is going to keep me from going to worship God. I am going to put him first in my life."

Some time after that, on a Sunday morning, she was getting ready for worship, and she noticed that he was getting ready also. He went to worship with her that morning and stood outside the building. He listened from outside, and when the invitation song was sung, he went inside, walked down the aisle, and was baptized into Christ for the remission of his sins.

He spent the rest of his life in faithful service to the Lord. One of their children was my grandmother. More than twenty gospel preachers have come from my great grandmother's family. So many men are preaching the Good News about Jesus today because one godly, faithful woman made up her mind to go to worship, regardless of the cost.

Occasionally, someone will ask, "Is it really important to attend worship? Do I have to attend all the services of the church?" When I think about people who choose to stay away from worship because of a sporting event, a school activity, to go hunting, fishing, or golfing, or because visitors are coming into town, they're tired from working all day, they want to watch some television show, or a long list of other excuses that people give, it is both mind-boggling and heartbreaking.

Will we really choose to miss the opportunity to encourage and edify others by being together (Heb. 10:24–25)? Is it worth missing out on a chance to grow in our walk with God (1 Pet. 2:2; 2 Pet. 3:18) by failing to attend Bible study or worship? What about showing our love to the Lord for what he has done for us (1 John 4:19)?

We are not talking here about people who are sick, shut-in, or because of some legitimate reason can't attend worship and Bible study. We are talking about people who choose to place other things or people above the Lord. We are talking about people who claim that they love Jesus, but allow anything and everything to keep them away from worship.

Christian friend, may I encourage you to think seriously about your attitude toward worshiping and studying with God's people? There are people who attend that can benefit greatly from your encouragement. The church needs your presence. You need to be with other Christians in a worship setting. You need to study God's Word with the church. You need to express your gratitude to Christ for all that he has done for you. You need to feast at the table of the Lord with your Savior and with his people.

Dear Father in heaven, please help us to think soberly about our attitudes about worshipping with your people. Help us, dear God, to show our love for you and our concern for others by choosing to worship with the church. Father, help us to know that our presence is a great source of encouragement and strength to others. May we understand that one of the ways we can grow in our faith is by being present when your people have gathered. In Jesus' name, Amen.

MY WEDDING RING IS STUCK

January 30, 2012

It had to be done. I had put it off for nearly three years. You know the procedure. That dreaded procedure that everyone is supposed to have when they turn fifty. It's that procedure where the prep is much worse than the actual procedure. The one where the sleep you get is some of the best sleep ever, but it's way too short. Well, I got that news from the doctor that everyone wants to hear. "I'll see you in ten years!"

When the anesthesiologist came in, he asked me if I could take off my wedding ring. I kept trying, but it just wouldn't come off. They gave me some special liquid to try, but it still wouldn't budge. I had to sign a special release to be able to have the procedure while wearing my ring.

I started thinking about how long it had been since my wedding ring had been off my finger, and I don't think I've had it off since the day Laura placed in on my finger more than thirty years ago. Of course the problem is I've put on a few pounds since the day we married. I'm working diligently this year to shed a few of those, but I don't have any plans to remove my ring. It is permanently stuck.

We live in a time when way too many of God's people are taking off their wedding rings. How can we reverse the current trend? How can we stop the rising divorce rate among the people of God? What are the characteristics needed to ensure that our wedding rings would be forever stuck? Let's consider just a few.

Commitment. When God brought the first couple together he said, "Therefore a man shall leave his father and his mother and hold fast to his wife, and they shall become one flesh" (Gen. 2:24). The idea presented here is that, when a man and a woman are joined together in marriage, they are to be close to one another for a lifetime. If we do not have this type of commitment, we will quit the first time trouble comes along.

Calling. Marriages will be strong when a husband and wife understand the role to which God has called them. When a man loves his wife the way Christ loves the church (Eph. 5:25, 28), and when he leads her the way Christ leads the church, happiness will prevail. When a wife lives in submission to her husband the way the church lives in submission to Christ (Eph. 5:22), marriages will be strong.

Coaching. Our wedding rings will remain stuck when we are willing to receive advice and help from others. The strongest couples surround themselves with other faithful couples that will encourage and strengthen. The kind of people we associate with will influence our marriages (1 Cor. 15:33). We should consider those among us who have been married successfully for many years. We don't need to look for perfect marriages—there are none—but we would do well to look for faithful marriages to emulate.

Caring. When a husband and wife care deeply about each other and their marriage, they will work to keep the wedding bands stuck. We need to show our care and concern for one another as the years roll on. It is important during every phase of marriage that husbands and wives show each other how much they care. When the Word of God commands us to be kind to one another (Eph. 4:32), surely that would include our spouse.

I thank God that my wedding ring is stuck and I hope yours will be as well. My prayer is that they become a permanent part of who we are, that they help define us. Good, strong marriages take a lot of effort, a lot of prayer, and a lot of time. With God's help and our work, we can build strong families that will be an influence for good through many years.

Dear Father in heaven, help us to build the kind of marriages that will keep our wedding rings stuck. Help us, Lord, to show our children and others around us what real marriages should be. Dear God, may we be the kind of person that both desires and works to make sure our marriages are strong. In Jesus' name, Amen.

DON'T THINK ABOUT IT

January 4, 2011

While on a recent flight to speak in Palm Beach Lakes, Florida, I picked up the Delta magazine and thumbed through it. An article entitled "Philosopher's Stone" caught my eye. The article was about the film *127 Hours*, the story of Aaron Ralston who got his hand stuck between a boulder and a canyon wall in Utah while climbing in 2003. After five days with barely any food or water, he decided to perform a backcountry arm amputation to survive. Ralston wrote about his experience in 2006 in his book, *Between a Rock and Hard Place*. Danny Boyle became obsessed with the story and decided to make the movie.

There was a quote in this article from Boyle that caused me to think about where we are as a society and, to a large degree, what seems to be happening in the church. Boyle said, "I'm not really a philosopher, I've got to be honest, I'm a visceral man. I want you to feel the film. I don't want you to think about the film intellectually…"

That statement presents a real conundrum for me. One of the reasons I don't go to movies very often is because I don't want to think intellectually. But I also don't want to "feel deeply. " It seems that most of my life is comprised either of "thinking intellectually," or "feeling deeply." So my thought is, I don't want to do that during my down time.

Having said that it seems that this is a caricature of where we are in our society, and as I said earlier, it seems this is where we are in the church. Perhaps there have been times in the history of the church when some have attempted to stifle feeling and emotion. When feeling is taken out of our faith, it causes great harm to our walk with the Lord.

The Word of God speaks openly about the need for heart in our spiritual walk. Jesus told a wealthy young man that he needed to love God with all of his heart, as well as his soul and mind (Luke 10:27). He also commanded us to worship God in "spirit and in truth" (John 4:24). If an individual can bow at the cross of Jesus without any emotion, there is a problem somewhere.

The problem in our day seems to be the other side of the coin. While there seems to be more heart, is it possible that we have excluded the head? Have we developed a religion that says, "Don't think about it intellectually; just feel it?" We must remember that the same Jesus who said, "Love the Lord your God with all your heart," also said, "...with all your mind" (Matt. 22:37). He also said, "You will know the truth, and the truth will set you free" (John 8:32).

Brethren, can't we be more balanced? Can't we find a happy medium? Can't we think intellectually and feel deeply at the same time? Jesus looked at those he loved, and he wept about their spiritual condition. He loved them and taught them.

When we worship the Lord, we should use both head and heart. We should use our head to assure that we are worshipping in a way that pleases God. We should use our heart to help us praise him and bring glory to him.

Preachers, can't we "preach the truth in love" (Eph. 4:15)? It seems we sometimes find ourselves between a rock and a hard place. We desperately need to find the balance between head and heart. We need to help our brothers and sisters find this balance as well. Our world needs to see Christians who think deeply about Scripture and Christians who feel deeply about what it means to be a Christian.

Dear Father in heaven, help us to be balanced in our approach to Scripture, as well as our approach to our walk with you. Help us to think about what your Word teaches, and help us to feel deeply about our commitment to you. Dear God, forgive us when we have failed you an those around us. Help us to love you more, and help us to live in such a way that we glorify you every day. In Jesus' name, Amen.

CHOOSE YOU
THIS DAY

C hoose Life."
    "Choose the church of your choice."

"It's your choice."

"The choice is clear."

In our society choice is important. Freedom of choice has become one of our great American privileges. There are many choices we will make in our lifetime. Some of our choices have little or no consequences. Some of our choices are life changing. The most important choice we will ever make is the one Joshua called upon the people of God to make some 3,500 years ago.

Bob Dylan wrote a song in 1968 with the title "You've Gotta Serve Somebody." Whether he realized the depth of these words may be left for discussion, but he was right on target when he said, "You may serve the devil, or you may serve the Lord. But everybody's got to serve somebody." When Joshua spoke to the people of Israel, he informed them that their choice was between the false gods they had created, or the true God of Israel who delivered them from bondage. They could easily recall what God had done for them. They had previously been encouraged to remember that it was God who had brought them to the Promised Land. They had been told to remember that it was God who gave them every blessing that they enjoyed (Deut. 6:10–23).

Ultimately, we have the same choice. Our choice is between God and Satan. We also have been reminded that it is God who created us (Acts 17:24–25), it is God who has redeemed us (1 Pet. 1:18–19), and it is God who has blessed us abundantly (Eph. 1:3; Jas. 1:17). Like God's people of long ago, we too have been rescued from a hard taskmaster. We were slaves to sin, but by his mighty hand, he brought us to freedom.

In order that we might make the proper choices throughout our lives, there are some crucial questions that need to be asked. Do the choices I make glorify God? The psalmist prayed, "Let the words of my mouth and the meditation of my heart be acceptable in your sight, O LORD, my rock and my redeemer" (Psa. 19:14). The choices I make every day must reflect the fact that my mouth will speak nothing but those things which are truthful, kind, and beneficial. "Let no corrupting talk come out of your mouths, but only such as is good for building up, as fits the occasion, that it may give grace to those who hear" (Eph. 4:29).

My heart must meditate on nothing but things that are holy, pure, and virtuous. A long time ago, a wise king said, "Keep your heart with all vigilance, for from it flow the springs of life" (Prov. 4:23). That same king also said, "For as he thinks in his heart, so is he" (Prov. 23:7 NKJV). An even wiser King came into the world and said, "For where your treasure is, there will your heart be also" (Luke 12:34).

We make many choices in life, but we must first ask, "Will my choices glorify God? The apostle Paul wrote, "So, whether you eat or drink, or whatever you do, do all to the glory of God" (1 Cor. 10:31). In all our choices and plans for life, let all that we do be done to the glory of God. Let us make spiritual and godly choices so that we can say with Jesus, "I glorified you on earth, having accomplished the work that you gave me to do" (John 17:4).

Will my choices help me to grow spiritually? "The righteous flourish like the palm tree and grow like a cedar in Lebanon" (Psa. 92:12). The nature of this tree is that it is always green and yielding a sweet smell. We must grow nearer to heaven with each choice that we make. With a holy ambition, we must make choices that prove our desire for that better world. What about my choices? Will doing these things improve my spiritual life? Will they encourage godliness? Will they build me up spiritually? "Like newborn infants, long for the pure spiritual milk, that by it you may grow up into salvation" (1 Pet. 2:2). "But grow in the grace and knowledge of our Lord and Savior Jesus Christ. To him be the glory both now and to the day of eternity. Amen" (2 Pet. 3:18).

Too often, Christians make choices that hinder (rather than help) their spiritual growth. The author of the book of Hebrews discussed the importance of discernment in the choices that we make. "

> For though by this time you ought to be teachers, you need someone to teach you again the basic principles of the oracles of God. You need milk, not solid food, for everyone who lives on milk is unskilled in the word of righteousness, since he is a child. But solid food is for the mature, for those who have their powers of discernment trained by constant practice to distinguish good from evil.
>
> — Heb. 5:12–14

Will my choices do anything to defile my body? Our body is the temple of the Holy Spirit of God. Paul wrote, "Do you not know that your body is a temple of the Holy Spirit within you, whom you have from God? You are not your own, for you were bought with a price. So glorify God in your body" (1 Cor. 6:19–20). Our soul and body must be used in the service of our Maker. Paul wrote, "Do not present your members to sin as instruments for unrighteousness, but present yourselves to God as those who have been brought from death to life, and your members to God as instruments for righteousness" (Rom. 6:13). We must serve God with our head, heart, hands, feet, and our entire body (Rom. 12:1–2). God expects us to be holy inside and out. The decisions you make as to how to use your body should always reflect your desire to honor Jesus Christ.

Will my decisions bring me into some form of slavery? How many times has someone said there is nothing wrong with a little social drinking, but before long, they become an alcoholic? Millions across the world are slaves to liquor. Someone smokes that first cigarette or takes that first dip, and soon they are a slave to tobacco. Many are slaves to gambling and the thrill it brings them. There are all kinds of chemical addictions that take control of individuals. Others are slaves to over-eating, too much television or computer games. Still others find themselves addicted to fornication, pornography, homosexuality or other sexual sins. Paul said, "All things are lawful for me,' but not all things are helpful. 'All things are lawful for me,' but I will not be dominated by anything" (1 Cor. 6:12). If what you are considering can be a destructive habit, why pursue it? We are to be a bond-servants of the Lord Jesus Christ, and him alone.

> So you also must consider yourselves dead to sin and alive to God in Christ Jesus. Let not sin therefore reign in your mortal body, to make you obey its passions. Do not present your members to sin as instruments for unrighteousness, but present yourselves to God as those who have been brought from death to life, and your members to God as instruments for righteousness. For sin will have no dominion over you, since you are not under law but under grace. What then? Are we to sin because we are not under law but under grace? By no means! Do you not know that if you present yourselves to anyone as obedient slaves, you are

slaves of the one whom you obey, either of sin, which leads
to death, or of obedience, which leads to righteousness?

— Rom. 6:11–16

Will my choices help the cause of Christ to grow? The choices that
we make in our life will largely determine whether you will be a soul
winner or not. Paul wrote, "For I am not ashamed of the gospel, for
it is the power of God for salvation to everyone who believes, to the
Jew first and also to the Greek" (Rom. 1:16). The world is watching
us. What do my decisions say about my faith in God? We must be
careful not to give any unconverted person a reason to be prejudice
against Christianity. Your life should reflect your concern for a lost
world. "In the same way, let your light shine before others, so that
they may see your good works and give glory to your Father who is
in heaven" (Matt. 5:16). Godly choices open the door for powerful
evangelistic work. Jesus said, "Go into all the world and proclaim the
gospel to the whole creation. Whoever believes and is baptized will
be saved, but whoever does not believe will be condemned" (Mark
16:15–16).

The choices we make will also largely determine whether or not
we will be one who encourages or tears down the Body of Christ.
Jesus said that we are to love one another, and it is by our love that
the world will know we belong to him (John 13:34–35). Each of the
following "one another" passages can only be obeyed if we make the
right choices.

- "Love one another with brotherly affection. Outdo one
  another in showing honor" (Rom. 12:10).
- "So then let us pursue what makes for peace and for
  mutual upbuilding" (Rom. 14:19).
- "May the God of endurance and encouragement grant
  you to live in such harmony with one another, in

accord with Christ Jesus, that together you may with one voice glorify the God and Father of our Lord Jesus Christ" (Rom. 15:5-6).

- "That there may be no division in the body, but that the members may have the same care for one another" (1 Cor. 12:25).

- "For you were called to freedom, brothers. Only do not use your freedom as an opportunity for the flesh, but through love serve one another" (Gal. 5:13).

- "Bear one another's burdens, and so fulfill the law of Christ" (Gal. 6:2).

- "With all humility and gentleness, with patience, bearing with one another in love" (Eph. 4:2).

- "Be kind to one another, tenderhearted, forgiving one another, as God in Christ forgave you" (Eph. 4:32).

- "Bearing with one another and, if one has a complaint against another, forgiving each other; as the Lord has forgiven you, so you also must forgive" (Col. 3:13).

- "May the Lord make you increase and abound in love for one another and for all, as we do for you" (1 Thess. 3:12).

- "Now concerning brotherly love you have no need for anyone to write to you, for you yourselves have been taught by God to love one another" (1 Thess. 4:9).

- "Therefore encourage one another and build one another up, just as you are doing" (1 Thess. 5:11).

- "But exhort one another every day, as long as it is called 'today,' that none of you may be hardened by the deceitfulness of sin" (Heb. 3:13).

- "Let us consider how to stir up one another to love and good works, not neglecting to meet together, as is the habit of some, but encouraging one another, and all the more as you see the Day drawing near" (Heb. 10:24–25).

- "Having purified your souls by your obedience to the truth for a sincere brotherly love, love one another earnestly from a pure heart" (1 Pet. 1:22).

- "Finally, all of you, have unity of mind, sympathy, brotherly love, a tender heart, and a humble mind. Do not repay evil for evil or reviling for reviling, but on the contrary, bless, for to this you were called, that you may obtain a blessing" (1 Pet. 3:8–9).

- "Above all, keep loving one another earnestly, since love covers a multitude of sins" (1 Pet. 4:8).

Will my choices violate my conscience? Once I have said or done this, will I feel miserable, unhappy and guilty? A clean conscience is of great value. My relationship with God can never be right as long as I am violating my conscience. Paul wrote, "Whoever has doubts is condemned if he eats, because the eating is not from faith. For whatever does not proceed from faith is sin" (Rom. 14:23). If you are considering doing something, and it bothers your conscience, then you should avoid doing, saying or thinking that thing. "Whenever our heart condemns us, God is greater than our heart, and he knows everything" (1 John 3:20). We cannot expect to have peace in life if we are doing things that violate our conscience. As Christians, we must live so that our hearts will not condemn us for any secret sin. God is greater than our heart, and he knows all things.

Will my choices help me to become more like Jesus? It is true that Jesus came into the world to save the lost (Luke 19:10). He was here to die upon the cross, and he was focused on that choice (Luke 9:51, 53). However, he also came into this world to teach us how to live. "For to this you have been called, because Christ also suffered for you, leaving you an example, so that you might follow in his steps" (1 Pet. 2:21). Paul told the Corinthian Christians that they should follow him in the same way that he followed Christ (1 Cor. 11:1). His prayer for the Galatian Christians was that Christ would be "formed" in them (Gal. 4:19).

Will my choices fulfill my purpose for being on earth? You must ask yourself, "Will my choices please God and fulfill his purposes for my life?" We read in 1 Corinthians 10:32-33, "Give no offense to Jews or to Greeks or to the church of God, just as I try to please everyone in everything I do, not seeking my own advantage, but that of many, that they may be saved." Our ultimate purpose for being on earth is to go to heaven and to encourage others to go too. I should never make a decision that will cause either me or someone else to stumble. We must never do anything that would cause another person to stumble. If we cause a brother or sister to stumble in their faith, we sin against Christ. "Thus, sinning against your brothers and wounding their conscience when it is weak, you sin against Christ" (1 Cor. 8:12)

When Joshua said, "Choose this day whom you will serve..." he was challenging the people of God to make the proper choice. We are constantly challenged to make proper choices throughout our life. The most important choice we will ever make is when we choose to follow Christ. Our Savior said in Luke 9:23, "If anyone would come after me, let him deny himself and take up his cross daily and follow me." The call to follow Jesus involves three distinct imperatives.

The first is self-denial. The meaning of the word Jesus uses suggests that something must be disowned. Jesus is saying we must disown ourselves if we are going to follow him.

The second requirement has to do with cross-bearing. When Jesus spoke of bearing your cross, he was not talking about what many today understand when we say, "well, we all have our crosses to bear." When those who were with Jesus heard him say that we must bear a cross, they immediately thought of death. They understood that Jesus meant, "If you are going to follow me, it means you are willing to die with me if necessary."

The third requirement is obedience. Our Lord concluded this call with the words, "Follow me." Jesus is talking about constant and complete obedience. We must continually obey Christ, and we must obey everything that he says. Therefore, it is true, the greatest choice we will ever make in our lives is the choice to follow Christ.

Dear God, help us today to make choices that will glorify you, that will help us grow in our walk with you, and that will help us be closer to Jesus. Help us realize that the choices we make today will affect us in the future. In Jesus' name we pray, Amen.

LESSONS
FROM HARRY

March 17, 2011

On Thursdays when I am in town, it is my privilege to conduct a Bible study at the retirement home across the street from our building. Each week, the crowd is different. But from the first week I was involved, there has been one constant: Harry.

Harry seems to be in charge. On occasions, he wears a name badge that says "President." One time, I asked Harry what he was president of, and he said, "All this!"

Harry is a delightful man. He has a robust laugh and seems to genuinely enjoy life. Today, I went to the retirement home for our Bible study and no one showed up but Harry. He told me that there was a meeting going on about what everyone needed to do in case of a disaster (tornado, fire, etc.). He said, "They tell you the same thing at every meeting, and I think I've got it down now"—Harry is 85—"besides that I'm not going to miss Bible study!"

Since no one else showed up, Harry and I just visited for nearly an hour. He told me about his life; he had grown up in south Texas and worked for many years for GE in Houston. He told me about attending a football game in the 1950s when a Texas A&M team coached by Bear Bryant beat a good Rice team. He talked about his children and grandchildren, all of whom make him very proud. I asked Harry what he likes to do with his time these days. He said he watches a little TV until it gets too bad ("which," he said, "doesn't take too long"), and he loves to look at train magazines. I asked Harry where he got his love for trains, and he said he once worked for the railroad.

Harry then seemed to become pensive and said, "I guess I'm what you call one of those 'loners.' Most of my co-workers and friends have passed away, and all my family lives a long way off."

During the course of our conversation, numerous people walked by the seating area where we were visiting. Harry took the time to greet every person, and he asked each one if they wanted to join our Bible study. Allow me to share a few lessons I learned today from my friend Harry that would be good for all Christians.

Be kind to everyone. Some of the people Harry greeted he called by name. I know Harry didn't know everyone who walked by because more than once after speaking he would say, "I don't know who that is!" Then he would laugh. The Bible speaks often of the kindness of God (Rom. 2:4; 11:22; Eph. 2:7; Tit. 3:4; 1 Pet. 2:3), as well as the need for his people to be kind (2 Cor. 6:6; Gal. 5:22; Col. 3:12; 2 Pet. 1:7). If we really want to be more like Jesus, we will be kind to everyone.

Invite others to church. Harry must have invited thirty people or more to join us today. I thought about all the people we see every day and wondered how many we invite to join us for worship. Friendship Evangelism is one of the greatest methods of sharing the gospel with others. God's people should want to tell others the Good News. Like Paul, we should not be "ashamed of the gospel" (Rom. 1:16).

Love life. Harry could easily get down about his plight in life, but he genuinely loves life. His joy is contagious. I noticed a number of people who smiled when Harry spoke to them. Even when he spoke briefly of being a "loner," Harry would not dwell on it, nor allow it to control him. Of all people who should love life, it should be the people of God. We are a redeemed people, purchased with the blood of Jesus (1 Cor. 6:19–20). We have an abundance of spiritual blessings in Christ (Eph. 1:3). Our Savior has given us an abundant life (John 10:10). Our life should be characterized by joy (Phil. 4:4).

Spend quality time with wise people who have experienced life. I get the feeling Harry has seen a little bit of everything. He certainly seems to have a lot of wisdom from what he has experienced. Moses prayed that God would "teach us to number our days that we may get a heart of wisdom" (Psa. 90:12). Solomon said that one of the purposes for the writing of Proverbs was so that we would know wisdom (Prov. 1:2) He further says we are to be attentive to wisdom (Prov. 2:2), we are to acquire wisdom (Prov. 4:5, 7), and that we will be blessed if we find wisdom (Prov. 3:13). One of the best ways to gain wisdom is by spending time with older people who are also wise. Age alone does not bring wisdom, but when one has lived a wise life, there is much we can learn.

Today we didn't have our usual Bible study in which I taught the class. Rather, I listened and was taught by a wise man, my friend, "President Harry!"

Dear Father, help us to be kind to everyone we see. Help us to exemplify Jesus with our lives. Help us, dear God, to share the Good News with as many people as we possibly can. Father, may we gain wisdom from those around us who have lived life to the fullest. Help us to love life and to be thankful for the abundant life Jesus gives. In his name, Amen.

WHAT HE DIDN'T DO

November 12, 2011

The eyes of our nation have been fixed this week on the campus of Penn State University. By now, everyone has read, heard, or seen numerous accounts of the tragic events that have been chronicled throughout the week related to the Jerry Sandusky scandal. There have been allegations, arrests, firings, protests, riots, and a general sense of unbelief. How could something like this happen in such a storied football program? I don't remember in my lifetime a sports story ever given this much press. There have been allegations that a popular assistant coach has sexually abused young boys and allegations that the football program, as well as the university, turned a blind eye.

At the center of it all is the legendary coach, Joe Paterno. For the first time in more than forty years, Coach Joe is not the head coach of the Nittany Lions. "JoePa" was an outstanding college football coach. He was the head coach at Penn State for 46 years and won more games than any other college coach. I remember attending the 1979 Sugar Bowl when the Crimson Tide beat him and his team. It was a classic game coached by two of the nations greatest football minds.

The question that has been asked over and over again by the talking heads is what kind of legacy will Paterno have now that these events have occurred? One former coach said that Paterno's legacy would be forever tarnished by what he didn't do. Please remember that we still do not know exactly what Paterno knew or didn't know. We do not know all that he did, or did not do. However, he has stated that, in hindsight, he wishes he could have done more.

Haunting words. A legacy forever tarnished by what he didn't do. I wonder how many people in the world could say those very words, "I wish I would have done more."

Jesus talked about how there will be many who will miss heaven because of what they didn't do. They didn't feed the hungry, they didn't give drink to the thirsty, they didn't accept the stranger, and they didn't care for the sick, the poor, or those in prison. Our Lord said that refusing to do so for others was tantamount to refusing to do for him (Matt. 25:41–46).

James, the brother of our Lord, once said, "So whoever knows the right thing to do and fails to do it, for him it is sin" (Jas. 4:17). We tend to want to focus on what we do, but today, I'm wondering about what we have failed to do?

I wonder about Christians who fail to tell others the Good News about Jesus and how he saves (1 Cor. 9:16; Rom. 1:16).

I wonder about preachers who fail to proclaim the whole counsel of God because they are afraid they will lose popularity (Gal. 1:10; Acts 20:27).

I wonder about elders who fail to do the right thing in the church because they are afraid they'll lose members or money (1 Cor. 9:16).

I wonder about parents who fail to raise their children in the discipline and the instruction of the Lord (Eph. 6:1–4).

I wonder about parents who fail to teach their children the Word of God, but they want to make sure they are properly educated (Deut. 6:1–9).

I wonder about parents who fail to teach their children to put God first by the way they put just about anything and everything above the Lord (Matt. 6:33).

I wonder about grown children who fail to honor and respect their parents because of their own selfish desires (Eph. 6:1–2).

I wonder about members of the church who fail to worship with God's people because they have something better to do (Heb. 10:22–25).

I wonder about Christians who fail to give as they should because they don't trust the Lord to take care of them (Luke 6:38).

I wonder about Christian young people who fail to say no to drugs, drinking, or some other immoral activity because they are afraid of losing friends (1 Cor. 15:33).

I wonder about churches that fail to show compassion for the disenfranchised, but they are obsessed with making sure we "preach the truth" (Matt. 23:23).

I wonder about churches that fail to "preach the truth," but they are obsessed with helping the disenfranchised (2 Tim. 4:1–4).

I wonder about churches that fail to see that it is possible to grow and "preach the truth" at the same time (Eph. 4:15).

I wonder if our failures will cause our spiritual legacy to be tarnished forever. On that day when we stand before our Lord, will he say, "Well done" because of what we have done? Or will he say, "Depart from me," because of what we have failed to do?

Dear Father in heaven, help us not to tarnish our spiritual legacy by what we fail to do. Help us to do right when we know the right thing to do. Help us to try harder each day to be like our Savior who went about doing good. In his name, Amen.

WHAT I CAN'T LIVE WITHOUT

February 22, 2010

This morning, I took my MacBook Air to the Apple Store to be sent off for repairs. The hinge on the back is coming apart. They agreed to repair it at no charge and told me it would likely be delivered to my house by Friday. I told the very nice young lady at the Genius Bar that I wasn't sure I could do without it that long. She just smiled and said, "I bet you'll be just fine."

So I'm working with Laura's laptop until my MacBook Air returns. It's been four hours now, and I already miss it. Her laptop must weight all of five pounds. My favorites aren't locked in on the web browser. This is awful!

I've been thinking about what I told the young lady at the Apple Store, "I don't know if I can do without it..." Who am I kidding? I'll be fine if I never see that computer again—at least that's what I keep telling myself! I'll be fine if I lose all its data. There is much in my life that I could live without. However, there are a few things in my life I hope and pray I don't ever have to live without.

I don't want to live without my Lord. Jesus makes such a tremendous difference in our lives that we cannot possibly exist without him. Jesus makes it possible for us to do all things (Phil. 4:13). He makes all spiritual blessings possible (Eph. 1:3). Jesus intercedes for us when we go to the Father (1 Tim. 2:5). He brings peace to our hearts (Rom. 5:1; Col. 3:15). Jesus brings light into our world and enlightens every man (John 1:9). Jesus has promised us that he will not leave us or forsake us (Matt. 28:20). We can choose to separate ourselves from him, but our lives will be fruitless if we do.

I don't want to live without God's Word. God's Word is a comfort to us in times of trouble. God's Word is a light for the pathway of life (Psa. 119:105). It keeps us from sin (Psa. 119:11). God's Word instructs us, corrects us, and equips us (2 Tim. 3:16–17). We are richly blessed to be able to study and know God's Word, yet many refuse to avail themselves of the great blessings contained in the Word of God.

I don't want to live without my wife. My sweet Laura has stood beside me for nearly thirty years. We have been through so much together, and she has made the burdens of life easier to bear. More than anyone else in the world, she taught me about the importance of family. She helped me become a better husband and father, a better preacher, a better man, a better friend, and a better Christian. I can't imagine life without her. I thank God for her everyday.

I don't want to live without my children. Amanda and Jeremy have brought, and continue to bring, so much joy into our lives. They have been a blessing to us from the time they entered the world. We are now blessed to watch them share life with their own mates, and we are extremely proud of both of them. We are most thankful that they, along with their mates, are faithful to the Lord and his cause. We pray daily that this will always be the case. I can't imagine a life without either of them.

I don't want to live without the church. The Body of our Lord has blessed my life in ways that are too numerous to count. We have had the privilege of working with four congregations during the past thirty years. Each of them has been unique, and each of them has blessed us. We have worked with wonderful elderships and great co-workers in the Kingdom. We have been treated wonderfully by every church we have been with during our ministry. We still have close friends in all of the congregations we have served. They have all taught us and helped us be more of what God wants us to be. The churches where we have worked have stood behind us and been patient with our weaknesses. We feel extremely blessed to work now with the Lewisville church. We are convinced that it is one of the great congregations of God's people in the world.

I don't want to live without my friends. My life has been blessed with more wonderful friends than I deserve. My closest friends in the world are preachers. I love preachers, and I love to be associated with them. There are a number of preachers that I could call at any moment and they would drop everything to come to my aid. I would do the same for them. I love the older preachers who continue to bless my life. I love the younger preachers who are receiving the baton from the older guys. We have some wonderful friends who are special to us during the empty-nest season of life. I have friends who are still close from high school and college days. How blessed a man is who has friends.

There are many things in this life I can live without. However, there are some things in this life that I hope I never have to live without. My list is not exhaustive, but these are a few that have been on my mind today. What's on your list?

Dear God, please help us not to get so caught up in the temporary things of this life. Please forgive us when we foolishly focus on things that don't matter. Father, help us to focus on the people in our lives that matter the most. Help us to express our thanks to those around us for influencing our lives in good ways. Thank you, Father, for the tremendous blessings of life that you constantly shower upon us. In Jesus' name, Amen.

WE STOOD &
APPLAUDED

July 9, 2011

I was sitting in the terminal at DFW early Friday morning, waiting to catch a flight to Alabama for a board meeting. Someone seated next to me stood and began to clap. I looked up and noticed soldiers walking out of the skyway on the concourse above us.

I stood and started clapping. An announcement came over the loud speaker saying, "Ladies and gentlemen, please welcome our troops returning home from Afghanistan today." Everyone in the terminal stood, applauded, and yelled. We stood for about fifteen minutes, everybody looking up, everybody applauding as hundreds of young men and women walked by. At times, the applause and yelling became deafening.

Tears began to well up in my eyes as I looked into their faces. I thought about how these brave men and women had given months or years of their lives to protect our freedoms. I thought about how they had been away from their families and all of the comforts we enjoy in this country. I thought about fellow soldiers they had lost in combat. I prayed, "Dear God, thank you for these wonderful men and women who have given so much for our country. Dear Father, please bless the loved ones of those who didn't come home. Father, help us to never take for granted what we enjoy so much."

Then I started thinking about others who need our applause. The Word of God teaches that we should give honor to those who deserve it (Rom. 13:7).

We should applaud parents who are committing time to raising their children in the nurture and admonition of the Lord; parents who spend time praying and studying with their children; parents who take time to make sure their families worship regularly with God's people and are involved in the life of the church.

We should applaud couples that are committed to one another. They should be commended for working through trials and difficulties to keep their families together.

We should applaud single parents who are courageously providing, physically and spiritually, for their families. These wonderful parents are doing the work of two parents.

We should applaud teenagers who are willing to stand out among their peers and say no to worldliness. These wonderful young people refuse to follow the crowd.

We should applaud college students across our land who are sometimes far from home, yet they continue to display Christian values learned from their parents.

We should applaud churches that remain committed to the truths of God's Word. We should applaud elders who will not be influenced by money or the threats of members to change the way they lead God's people. We should applaud these elders when they refuse to change just for the sake of growth. We should applaud elders when they shepherd the flock and when they focus on what is most important.

We should applaud deacons who are willing to serve so that elders may shepherd the church. We should applaud these men for having servant-hearts like Jesus.

We should applaud preachers when they proclaim the whole counsel of God. We should applaud them when they speak sound doctrine, even when it is unpopular. We should applaud them when they take time to study so that church members receive the proper nourishment.

We should applaud Sunday School teachers who spend hours preparing Bible lessons for our children. We should applaud them when they give up time to help our children learn the Word of God.

We should applaud those who have become the eyes, hands, and feet of Jesus to reach out to the less fortunate. We should applaud those who seek justice, righteousness, and mercy.

If we live in a way that is pleasing to God, he will honor us in this life, but most importantly in the life to come. He will say, "Well done, good and faithful servant..." (Matt. 25:21).

And that will be the greatest applause of all.

Dear God, may we be people who give honor to those who deserve it. Help us, dear God, not to praise ourselves but to seek to applaud others who do well. Help us, Father, to love those around us more and to love you more every day. In Jesus' name, Amen.

FINDING CONTENTMENT

May 16, 2012

Everybody loves the thought of being content. The difficulty is not desiring contentment; it is doing the hard work required to achieve contentment. One of our great difficulties is that we have lost the ability to distinguish between happiness and contentment. Doug Larson once said, "The world is full of people looking for spectacular happiness while they snub contentment."

The biblical idea of contentment is vastly different than the one that pervades our society. The word *content* itself only occurs five times in our Bibles, and the word *contentment* occurs only once. In 1 Tim. 6:6, Paul says, "But godliness with contentment is great gain." The word Paul uses here is *autarkeia*. It literally means, "a perfect condition of life in which no aid or support is needed." It is a reminder that we have the sufficiency of the necessities of life. In Paul's letter to Timothy, it is used to refer to the contentment of our minds.

Paul is trying to teach us that when our lives are characterized by godliness and contentment, we will live full, joyous lives. So the question is, how can we find this elusive mindset? What can we do to be certain that we have contentment as a part of who we are? While these suggestions are certainly not all-inclusive, our prayer is that they will be of some help as you search for this heavenly contentment.

Commune often with our Lord. There are three primary ways we can commune with our Lord. First, we can commune with him through the study of his Word. Our Lord has chosen to speak to us today through his Word. God speaks to us through his Son (Heb. 1:1), and we have the recorded Word of his Son, as well as those his Son commissioned in our New Testaments. Every time we read or study our Bibles, we are listening to God speak.

Paul admonished Christians, "Do not be conformed to this world, but be transformed by the renewal of your mind, that by testing you may discern what is the will of God, what is good and acceptable and perfect" (Rom. 12:2). One of the ways we can renew our minds is through study. Every time we open the Word of God, we learn more about the "unsearchable riches of Christ" (Eph. 3:8).

Another means of communing with our Lord is through prayer. Just as studying the Word is God's way of speaking to us, he has provided prayer as a means for us to communicate to him.

A while ago, Laura and I had the privilege of visiting with one of our dear sisters at Lewisville who was 96 years of age. It was just a few days before she passed away. At the time, her mind was still sharp, and I asked her if she had a favorite Bible passage. With very little thought she said, "Casting all your anxieties on him, because he cares for you" (1 Pet. 5:7). During her funeral, I used her Bible and was amazed at how many notes she had made about prayer. Here is a godly woman who had survived the loss of a husband and two sons to cancer. Even with all that she suffered, she seemed amazingly content with life. It was without a doubt due in large part to her life of prayer.

After all, the God who hears us is called the "God of all comfort" (2 Cor. 1:3). Knowing we have his comfort, as well as the "the peace of God, which surpasses all understanding" (Phil. 4:7), will help us to live lives of contentment.

Third, we can also commune with our Lord through worship. Jesus promised his disciples that he would commune with them in his Father's Kingdom (Matt. 26:29). Whenever we are gathered in worship, our Savior is present. We can be content in knowing that he is with us when we partake of his feast, when we pray to the Father through him, and when we bring glory to him through our worship.

The late beloved brother Hugo McCord told about meeting a man in Scotland who walked to church three miles every Sunday. He would worship and then walk the three miles back to his home. The brother was aging and did not enjoy the greatest health. Brother McCord said that he asked the brother why he put himself through this ordeal. His response was, "My Savior died for me, and I would never miss the opportunity to commune with him on Sunday!" What a wonderful example of a heart filled with contentment.

Compare ourselves only with Christ. Comparing is one of the favorite sports of Americans. We compare houses, cars, bank accounts, electronics, children, grandchildren, and just about everything else. When we are always comparing, we will never be content. The lesson Paul is attempting to teach us here is that comparing ourselves with others will always create a feeling of discontent. We should only compare our lives with Christ. He is our standard. He is our model. He left us "an example, so that you might follow in his steps" (1 Pet. 2:21). We are to do everything possible to develop his mind (Phil. 2:5). Our goal is to become more like him (Phil. 3:12–21).

Rather than gaining more stuff, we should work to simplify our lives. Jesus said, "One's life does not consist in the abundance of his possessions" (Luke 12:15). In a world where obtaining more stuff is the norm, Christians should work to be content with what we have. Our affections must not be set on the things that are on the earth, but rather on things that are of eternal significance (Col. 3:1-2). We must not store up for ourselves treasures on this earth, but rather treasures in heaven (Matt. 6:19–20).

In our text, Paul says, "But if we have food and clothing, with these we will be content" (1 Tim. 6:8). There are a number of statements in this section of Scripture to which we would loudly say, "Amen!" I don't remember ever hearing anyone say, "Amen!" when this verse is read. Most Christians in America would not likely be content if all we had was food and clothing.

Create opportunities for fellowship with other Christians. A great help in the preceding suggestion would be to spend a majority of time with people who have similar goals, dreams, and aspirations. It is true that we become like the people we spend time with, and the wrong type of associations can corrupt us (1 Cor. 15:33).

We cannot leave this world or refuse to associate with non-Christians (John 17), because we must do our part in taking the gospel to the world (1 Pet. 2:12). However, we must never place ourselves under the influence of people who do not follow Christ.

Those of us who have children should allow them to be influenced by other godly men and women. Paul said, "Be imitators of me, as I am of Christ" (1 Cor. 11:1). He also said, "Join in imitating me" (Phil. 3:17). The psalmist said that our children are gifts from God, and they are like arrows in the hand of a mighty warrior (Psa. 127:3–4). We are responsible for aiming our children in the right direction, and when we do, we can be content with the fact that we have done our job well.

Concentrate on the joys of being a Christian. Our world is filled with sorrow, sickness, suffering, and sin. If we are not careful, we will fall into the trap of living depressed and dejected lives. Jesus came to this world in part to bring us the abundant life (John 10:10). Only followers of Christ can truly understand this abundant living. We can rejoice always (Phil. 4:4). There's an old hymn that says, "Let the beauty of Jesus be seen in me. All his wonderful passion and purity..."

When we allow our lights to shine before men, they will see the beauty of Jesus and will glorify our Father who is in heaven (Matt. 5:16). Paul said to the Galatians that his prayer was that Jesus might be formed in them (Gal. 4:19). The joy that comes from knowing

Jesus should shine in our hearts (2 Cor. 4:6). When our focus in life is on the joy of Christian living, we will not only reach those around us, we will also be content throughout our lives.

Contentment from an eternal perspective will be ours when we commune regularly with our Lord, when we compare ourselves only to Christ, when we create opportunities for fellowship with other Christians, and when we concentrate on the joys of living the Christian life. May God help us to live every day with contentment from an eternal perspective.

Dear Father in heaven, we pray that we will become more content as we grow closer to you. Help us to commune often with you, help us to quit comparing ourselves to others, help us to create opportunities to fellowship with other Christians, and help us to concentrate on the joy we have in Christ. Thank you, dear God, for making it possible for us to live this life with an eternal perspective. In Jesus' name, Amen.

INSULTED

How do you handle it when you've been insulted? Maybe the insult is from someone who has something against you. Maybe it's shrouded in humor, but the insult is clear. Maybe it's from a well-meaning friend who says something innocently.

However, whenever and from whomever insults come, they always hurt. Whether true or false, insults hurt. The big question is how do we handle it when we've been insulted? How do we respond when someone insults us?

The wise writer of the Proverbs has some wonderful insight to help us out. He says, "The vexation of a fool is known at once, but the prudent ignores an insult" (Prov. 12:16). This statement is clear. Any fool can respond in haste and show anger when insulted. But it takes a wise individual to ignore an insult. It takes someone who refuses to jump at the chance to pay someone back. It takes a person with great patience to overlook it when someone says or does something that seems unkind.

It takes someone who is trying to live like Jesus. How did Jesus handle it when he was insulted? Peter, who witnessed it all, tells us what Jesus did. "When he was reviled, he did not revile in return; when he suffered, he did not threaten, but continued entrusting himself to him who judges justly" (1 Pet. 2:23). If we could learn to treat others like Jesus, to follow in his steps (1 Pet. 2:21) and to develop his mind (Phil. 2:5–8), we would be able to deal with insults so much better. Allow me to make just a few suggestions.

Look behind the anger. Many times, people insult us because they are angry with someone else. Perhaps someone has hurt them deeply, and they are just deflecting their pain toward us. It is often true that hurt people hurt people. If we can look behind the pain and anger of someone who has insulted us, it might help us to have a better understanding. We are not saying that another person's anger makes it all right to insult someone, but it might help us to understand just a little bit.

Practice self-control. We must come to grips with the reality that just because someone has insulted us does not give us the right to retaliate. Self-control is mentioned among the Christian graces (Gal. 5:23). Peter teaches us that it is one of the qualities that must be added to our lives if we want to be useful for Christ (2 Pet. 1:6) Self-control is required for men who desire to lead the church (2 Tim. 3:3).

Pray for wisdom. If we want to be able to deal with insults, we desperately need to pray for wisdom. The brother of our Lord teaches us that if we want wisdom, we should ask God (Jas. 1:5). The kind of wisdom needed to handle insults is "first pure, then peaceable, gentle, open to reason, full of mercy and good fruits, impartial and sincere" (Jas. 3:17).

Learn from insults and move on. There are times when we can learn lessons about ourselves from those who insult us. Even when someone attempts to do us harm, we should consider the fact that there could be something to what they are saying. If we can learn something, we should so that we might be more like Jesus. We might ask some close friend who will be honest with us if there is something we should learn from an insult.

Turn the problem and the person over to God. When we try to take matters into our own hands, we will always fall short. We are just not qualified to know another person's heart. Because of this, the best option is to pray about the matter and turn everything over to God. This is how Jesus handled it when he was insulted (1 Pet. 2:23). If Jesus needed to turn it over to God when he was insulted, what would make us believe that we can handle insults by ourselves? We need to spend a great amount of time in prayer when someone insults us so that we handle them in a way that will please God.

Dear God, when we feel insulted by others, help us to turn it over to you. Help us to follow the example of our Savior as we deal with insults in our life. Help us to consider what changes we need to make in our life, and please give us wisdom as we communicate with those around us. In Jesus' name, Amen.

FREEDOM!

October 15, 2010

"C hilean Miners Emerge to World Rejoicing." "Chili's Textbook Mine Rescue Brings Global Respect." Headlines like these appeared in every major newspaper in the world this week. After being trapped underground for 69 days, all 33 of the Chilean miners emerged to freedom. The whole world watched as, one by one, the miners were brought to safety.

My close friend, Steve Bailey, reminded me of some spiritual implications of the miner's experience. So with appreciation to Steve for his thoughts, and some additional thoughts of my own, here are a few comparisons between the experience of the Chilean miners and our own journey to freedom.

All of the men who worked in the mine were trapped. We live in a world where we are trapped by sin. James paints a picture of how we are enticed by lust, which leads to our being trapped in sin (Jas. 1:13–16).

The miners were separated from loved ones. For more than two months, they could not spend time with their families because of this terrible separation. The feeling of separation became nearly unbearable for some of the loved ones. Sin separates us from God and all that is good. The apostle Paul reminds us that, before we were set free, we "were at that time separated from Christ ... strangers to the covenants of promise, having no hope and without God in the world" (Eph. 2:12).

They could not save themselves. In spite of the fact that most of the miners were experienced in their work, once they were trapped, there was nothing they could do for themselves. Someone else had to come to their rescue. When we are trapped in sin, there is no way we can save ourselves. We can only be freed from sin if someone else comes to our rescue. Praise God that someone did, and that someone was Jesus (Luke 19:10). When we were helpless and hopeless, God loved us so much that he sent his Son to save us (John 3:16; Rom. 5:8).

The miners had to have faith. These men had to trust that those who built the Fenix capsule were trustworthy, and they had to have faith in the rescuers who came to the mine to help them. We cannot be saved without faith (Heb. 11:6). We must trust in the One who is the architect of our salvation, and we must have faith in the One who came to this world to bring us salvation (Heb. 12:1–3).

They had to act on their faith. No one would argue that these men saved themselves or that they were saved by their own work. However, it is evident that they had to do something to be saved. It did not matter how much faith they had in those who made their freedom possible, how much faith they had in those who came to help them, or how much they believed that the Fenix could bring them to freedom. Until they personally got into the Fenix, they would remain trapped. No one would argue that we could come up with a plan to save ourselves from sin, or that we can work enough to save ourselves. It doesn't matter how much faith we have in God who sent his Son to save us, or how much faith we have in Christ who came to rescue us—unless we are willing to do something, we will not be saved. Jesus said, "Whoever believes and is baptized will be saved, but whoever does not believe will be condemned" (Mark 16:16). We can no more be saved outside of Christ than the 33 miners could be saved outside of the Fenix. Their own works did not save them, but by the work of others, yet they still had to do something. We are not saved by our own works, but by the work of Christ, yet we still must do something (Acts 2:38). We must be "in Christ" (Rom. 6:3–4; Gal. 3:27), just as the Chilean miners had to be in the Fenix.

Their freedom was not free. The rescue of these men cost millions of dollars. In addition, thousands of hours of planning and implementation were put into their rescue. Our freedom from sin is not free. It cost the life and blood of the precious Son of God (1 Pet. 1:18–19).

The miners were rescued one man at a time. They could not all be rescued at once. Jesus came into this world to save each and every sinner. His concern is for us, personally and individually. We should be interested in helping each individual in the word obtain freedom.

They were brought from darkness to light. The miners were in darkness while underground, but they now are able to enjoy the light of day. Those who come to Christ are translated from the domain of darkness into the kingdom of Christ (Col. 1:13). Our Savior said, "Again Jesus spoke to them, saying, "I am the light of the world. Whoever follows me will not walk in darkness, but will have the light of life" (John 8:12).

What's next? Now that the Chilean miners have been rescued, they must consider what they will do with the rest of their lives. Will they go back to work and to their normal way of living? Will they write books to tell the world of their experience? Will they talk to their children and loved ones about how they were saved? Once we have been freed from sin, we have choices to make as well. We can live as if nothing has happened, or we can live as people who have been given a new, abundant life (John 10:10), and be faithful to our Lord until death (Rev. 2:10). We can keep our salvation to ourselves, or we can tell as many people as possible how we were rescued (Matt. 28:19–20). We can let our children/families learn it on their own, or we can share with them how God reached down from heaven into this dark world and made our salvation possible (cf. Deut. 6:20–24).

Dear Father in heaven, we thank you that these men are now free. We thank you that they have been reunited with their family and friends. We thank you that their long night of darkness has been replaced with the light of day. Dear God, we thank you most of all for the freedom that we have because of Christ. Thank you for sending Jesus into this dark world to bring light. Help us, Lord, to share the Good News of freedom with everyone we can. In Jesus' name, Amen.

HUMILITY

April 22, 2010

To speak or write about humility is a humbling experience. If you meet someone who presumed to know enough about it to speak on the topic, you might think they were disqualified. Preachers are often invited to speak for a church and are allowed the freedom to choose their own topic; on other occasions they are assigned a topic. I was recently asked to speak for a college retreat on the topic of humility. I would not have chosen that as my topic. One of the leaders of the retreat asked me to put some of the thoughts from my lesson on my blog. I do so at his request with great reservation in my mind. Please allow me to be clear from the beginning: I do not write these words as one who considers himself an authority on humility, but as a fellow pilgrim walking on a path set for us by our humble Savior. If you are interested in reading an excellent book on humility, I highly recommend C. J. Mahaney's *Humility: True Greatness.* Some of my thoughts for the presentation and for this article came from that book.

History, as well as contemporary examples, prove that humility will work in every area of life. Humility even attracts the world's notice at times. What's more astonishing, however, is that humility gets God's attention.

In Isa. 66:2, we read these words from the Lord, "But this is the one to whom I will look: he who is humble and contrite in spirit and trembles at my word." This should be our primary motivation and purpose for humility. Humility draws the attraction of our Sovereign God. If we could understand the background of this passage, we would see a rich meaning. God is addressing the Israelites, a people with a unique identity. They possessed both the house of God (the temple) and the law of God (the Torah), yet God says of them that they did not tremble at his Word. Like the children of God today, they had everything going for them except what was most important. They lacked humility before God.

We all want our Father's attention, and we want the grace of God. Did you know there is something you can do to receive more of God's grace? It is the same thing you do to receive God's attention. James 4:6 says that God gives grace to the humble. Contrary to popular belief, it's not those who help themselves that God helps. Rather, God helps those who humble themselves. Humility is needed and important.

What is humility? Mahaney defines it as "honestly assessing ourselves in light of God's holiness and our sinfulness." This is an outstanding definition. We will never fully humble ourselves until we understand who we are and who God is. We must evaluate ourselves honestly to see if we are growing in the humility that draws God's attention and attracts his grace.

If humility is our greatest need and greatest friend, pride is our greatest enemy. Pride is what happens when we fail to recognize the holiness of God and our own sinfulness. As much as God blesses and loves humility, he hates pride (Prov. 6:16–17). In Prov. 8:13, God says, "I hate pride and arrogance." In Prov. 16:5, the wise man says, "Everyone who is arrogant in heart is an abomination to the LORD; be assured, he will not go unpunished." Pride causes us to contend for supremacy with God. It can be seen in so many places: among the rich and poor, the educated and uneducated, the old and young.

Some confess pride, but they are not convicted concerning pride. In the same passage that says God gives grace to the humble, it also says he opposes the proud (Jas. 4:6). This verse indicates that God's opposition to pride is immediate and constant.

If there is going to be transformation in our lives, we must work to restrain pride and manifest humility. John Stott said, "In every step of our Christian growth and maturity, and throughout every aspect of our Christian obedience and service, our greatest foe is pride, and our greatest ally is humility." Every day, we should consider how we can weaken our greatest foe and strengthen our greatest enemy.

Please consider a few practical ways we can weaken pride and strengthen humility. I share them with you as a list. Please think of my list, not as requirements, but simply as recommendations. The goal here is not to promote some list of strict rules and regulations. These are for your reflection. After weighing their value, you need to custom-design your own list. Allow me to impress this on you. You should have a list. Each day, we should plan to defeat our greatest foe and cultivate our greatest friend.

Reflect regularly on the cross of Jesus. One cannot develop the wrong kind of pride while standing beneath the cross of our Lord. It was on the cross that our Savior exemplified humility at it's greatest. Paul reminds us, "he humbled himself by becoming obedient to the point of death, even death on a cross" (Phil. 2:8). The words to the old hymn say, "When I survey the wondrous cross, on which the Prince of Glory died, my richest gain I count but loss, and pour contempt on all my pride." Jesus was crucified on that cross because of me. It was both his love for me (John 3:16) and my sin that placed him there (Rom. 5:8). I cannot stand at the foot of the cross and develop an arrogant, self-serving attitude about my life.

Constantly acknowledge my need for God. The wise King Solomon said a long time ago, "In all your ways acknowledge him, and he will make straight your paths" (Prov. 3:6). Jeremiah understood perfectly our need for God when he declared, "I know, O LORD, that the way of man is not in himself, that it is not in man who walks to direct his steps" (Jer. 10:23). As highly as we may think of ourselves, we cannot make it through this life on our own. We must have the help of our loving Father. Peter knew exactly what he was talking about when he wrote, "Casting all your anxieties on him, because he cares for you" (1 Pet. 5:7).

Consistently recognize that God is the giver of all that is good. God is the Great Giver. He gives, as well as sustains, life (Acts 17:24–25). He gives us every good gift that we possess (Jas. 1:17). He gives us rich spiritual blessings (Eph. 1:3). God wants us to enjoy the blessings he showers upon us, yet he wants us to remember who gives them to us (Deut. 6:10–12).

Study God's Word daily. As we study the Word of God, we will see how much emphasis God places on humility in our lives. As we study the Bible, we will see how much he hates pride (Prov. 6:17). We will learn from the example of wonderful men and women of faith as we see how humility strengthened their lives or how pride destroyed them. Most importantly, we will witness the humility of Jesus, the greatest example of humility this world has ever seen. We should study the doctrines of sin and grace. These two great doctrines of Scripture will help us keep a proper view of God and ourselves. Some have convinced themselves that God's Word is outdated and that our advanced means of education is more important than Scripture. They believe we no longer need to study the Bible, rather we should listen to the "scholars."

Contemplate the attributes of God. The more we learn about God, the more we will recognize his greatness and our weakness. We should study his omniscience, omnipotence, and omnipresence. We should grow in our love for the sovereignty of our God. Most of all, we should grow in our knowledge of his holiness.

Learn to laugh. God has blessed us with the gift of laughter in a world filled with sadness. Jesus came so that we could live the abundant life (John 10:10). We will do well to surround ourselves with people who will bring joy and laughter to our souls. Our world is filled with so much sadness, and we should do what we can to find all the joy we possibly can find (Phil. 4:4).

Allow me to close with just a few comments to church leaders. I love preachers. Some of the greatest men I have ever known are preachers and elders. My closest friends through most of my life have been preachers. Brothers, it is vitally important that those of us who lead do our best to model humility. Some of the most humble men I have ever known are preachers. They do not boast and brag. They deflect credit away from themselves and direct it toward the Lord and others.

But sadly, some of the most arrogant men I have ever known are also preachers. They are always talking about what great things they have done or are doing. They view themselves as experts about seemingly everything. They set themselves up as the model for how to grow churches, how to raise families, how to train leaders, and a host of other topics. May God help us to always remember that he is the expert, and we are always the students; that he is responsible for the growth of churches and for everything good in our world.

Dear God, help us to humble ourselves daily before you. Help us recognize our sin and your holiness. Dear Father, please forgive our prideful, arrogant ways. Help us, Lord, to grow in humility as we follow our humble Savior. In his name, Amen.

WHEN LIFE DOESN'T WORK OUT

March 13, 2012

We spent months planning for the big day. We had prepared diligently. My brother, Dale, and I have been discussing the possibility of hosting a webinar for over a year. We finally decided to do it. We chose the theme, the date, and the venue. We spent months choosing the right host for the webinar. We worked a long time on the material we would present. We discussed the timing, the order, the intro, the conclusion, and every other aspect of the webinar we could imagine. We did a couple of trial runs, and everything seemed to be ready. We were both a little nervous, but we felt good that everything was going to work out just like we planned it.

To put it mildly, our first webinar was a colossal failure! We had Internet connection problems, problems with the company we had chosen to air the webinar, technical difficulties, sound issues, and basically everything that could have gone wrong, did! We were extremely disappointed. Fortunately, we were able to correct most of the issues, and we did something we had not planned on doing. We broadcast the live Webinar a second and a third time.

While all of the attendees were very patient and kind, we ultimately lost some of them. Some because of time issues, and some no doubt because of our problems. We hope to gain them back in future webinars. The lessons we learned were numerous.

I know that in the grand scheme of things, a webinar failure is small potatoes. I am also very aware of the fact that some of you who are reading this post are dealing with much larger issues.

The loss of a spouse, a report of some dreaded health issue, the loss of a child, the loss of a parent before you were ready to let them go, the loss of a job, huge financial concerns, a marriage that is not what you had dreamed it would be, children who have grown up and rejected what you taught them, church fights, being fired from a preaching position, seeing members disappoint you as you attempt to shepherd their souls, seeing church leaders with moral failures, dealing with people who are close to you who refuse to treat you kindly, and numerous other difficulties are all huge, real life issues that sometimes don't work out the way we had dreamed they would.

What do you do when you find yourself in one of these situations? Where do you turn? Who do you trust? How do you continue to live for the Lord when one or more of these issues slap you in the face?

Deepen your prayer life. There is no greater source of strength than our Father in heaven. He knows what it is like to deal with pain. He knows what it is like to handle disappointment. He knows how it feels to be hurt deeply by people you care about profoundly.

He calls upon us to give him our greatest struggles and concerns. "Casting all your anxieties on him, because he cares for you" (1 Pet. 5:7). God once said to his people, "Do not be afraid and do not be dismayed at this great horde, for the battle is not yours but God's" (2 Chron. 20:15).

We do not have to deal with the difficulties of life on our own. We have a heavenly Father who wants to help us, who is able to help us, and who longs to help us. We should continually call upon him.

Depend on other Christians. God has also blessed us with people here on the earth that can help us. There are many who have struggled with the same issues that you might be struggling with right now. There are many who have overcome the obstacles that would attempt to redefine the life of a Christian. We know that Satan is walking about on the earth trying to destroy Christians (1 Pet. 5:8), and we know he has powerful schemes. Yet many have overcome, and they are willing to help us overcome. God has put into place a network of people to help us.

Dig deeper into the Word. Another great resource that our great God has provided for us is his marvelous Word. Through reading the Word, we are given the opportunity to see how God's people dealt with difficulties in previous generations. God's Word gives us strength, comfort, power for daily living, and answers to some of life's most difficult questions. King David learned to love the Word of God (Psa. 119:97). He allowed the Word of God to guide him through life (Psa. 119:105).

Develop a greater trust in the Lord. While trusting in him certainly includes prayer and Bible study, there is more to it than those two wonderful activities.

Trust involves dependence. We must believe that God will be with us, that he will deliver us. We should depend on him more than anyone else. "Trust in the LORD with all your heart, and do not lean on your own understanding" (Prov. 3:5).

Trust involves acknowledgement. If we are going to handle the issues of life that don't turn out the way we had dreamed they would, then we must acknowledge that he is God and we are not. "In all your ways acknowledge him, and he will make straight your paths" (Prov. 3:6). The promise in this Scripture brings great hope when we feel that hope is lost.

Trusting in the Lord will make our lives happier. When we don't trust him, we are more likely to live in quiet desperation. Jeremiah 17:7 teaches us that we will be blessed if we trust in the Lord, and if the Lord is our trust.

When I think about a webinar failure, it pales in significance to so many big issues that people are struggling with. When you feel like life has let you down, there is great hope if you will deepen your prayer life, depend on fellow Christians to help you, dig deeper into the Word and develop a greater trust in the Lord.

Dear God, we thank you for being our trust when life seems hard. We pray that you will give us the strength to pray more, lean on others for help, find solace in your divine Word, and trust totally in you. Thank you, dear Lord, for all you do for us every day. Help us to love you more each day. In Jesus' name, Amen.

THE MATTHEW-MARK SONG

December 13, 2010

One of our favorite persons in our congregation is an outstanding young boy named Will. We have had the privilege of going to some of Will's birthday parties, and he always goes out of his way to give us a big hug at church. Last week, Will's parents asked if he could recite the books of the New Testament to me. On Sunday evening before our worship service, I met Will and his family in my office for Will to recite the books of the New Testament. Will did a flawless job singing the New Testament books. It was an honor to hear him sing. We were all so proud of him. By the way, Will's little sister also sung the New Testament books, with just a little help from her Mom.

Later after the evening service, Laura was talking to Will and said, "I heard you did something special tonight?" Will said, "Yes ma'am. " Here is the rest of their conversation:

Laura: "Did you say your ABC's?"

Will: "No ma'am."

Laura: "Did you count to 100?"

Will: "Nooo!"

Laura: "Did you tell him all of the Thomas the Train characters?"

Will: "Nooooo! I did the Matthew-Mark Song."

It is a tremendous blessing when parents teach their children the Word of God. When God's people were entering the Promised Land, he commanded them to teach their children. "These words that I command you today shall be on your heart. You shall teach them diligently to your children, and shall talk of them when you sit in your house, and when you walk by the way, and when you lie down, and when you rise" (Deut. 6:6–7).

We find the same type of instruction in the New Testament. The Holy Spirit says, "Fathers, do not provoke your children to anger, but bring them up in the discipline and instruction of the Lord" (Eph. 6:4). There are a couple of insights we can draw from these two great Scriptures.

First, in both of these passages, the emphasis is placed on the fact that Fathers should teach the children. Somewhere along the way, both as a society and as a church, we altered this God-ordained plan. We now seem to place the emphasis on mothers teaching the children. We are not saying here that mothers should not teach the Word to their children, but certainly God had a reason for placing this life-changing responsibility on dads!

The second thought from these passages is that God places a great importance on teaching content. The Deuteronomy text mentions statutes and commandments, as well as "these words." While it is wonderful to teach our children to recite the books of the Bible, it is more important that we teach them the lessons found in these marvelous books! In addition to this, it is crucial that we help our children learn about the God who authored these books.

In our worship this past Sunday morning, we studied Jude 20–21. In v. 20, Jude instructed our first brothers and sisters with these words, "building yourselves up in your most holy faith and praying in the Holy Spirit." The "most holy faith" refers to the gospel. This is the first approach that Jude gives to keeping ourselves in "the love of God" (v. 21). As you continue to grow in your own faith, and as you instruct your children in the "most holy Faith," here are a few thoughts that might be of some help.

Review the content of the gospel. We must grow in our knowledge of the Word of God (1 Pet. 2:2; 2 Pet. 3:18; Heb. 5:12–14). Peter's thought is that we must have an intense desire for God's Word. Every parent can understand this illustration of a child wanting milk. We all remember how our children would not quit crying until they got the milk they wanted. As children of God, we should have this same strong desire for the Word. How much time do you spend reading, meditating on, and studying the Word of God each week?

Rehearse the content of the gospel. It isn't enough to study the Bible if we do not put it into practice in our lives. The message of God's Word should transform everything about us. This is a life-changing message. Dr. Luke wrote all about what Jesus taught and did (Acts 1:1). There are many who know the Scriptures, but they refuse to live them. The apostle Paul stated in Phil. 4:9, "What you have learned and received and heard and seen in me—practice these things, and the God of peace will be with you." Some old-time preachers used to say, "You can have a head full of Scripture and heart full of sin at the same time." It isn't enough just to read and study Scripture; we must translate it into our life.

Rejoice in the content of the gospel every day. When God's Word is studied and translated into life, it brings great joy. Jesus wants his people to be joyful. He said that he had come to bring us "abundant life" (John 10:10). Scripture teaches us to always rejoice in the Lord (Phil. 4:4). When Christians live rejoicing lives, others will want to know more. Most people in our world live unfulfilled and unhappy lives. God has placed an eternal void in our hearts that can only be filled when we come to know him (Eccles. 3:11) Many attempt to fill this void with the wrong kinds of relationships, substance abuse, and a number of other lost causes. Our world desperately needs to see how Jesus changes lives and brings joy to our hearts!

Thank God for parents who are teaching children the importance of reviewing the gospel, rehearsing the gospel, and rejoicing in the gospel. There is no greater legacy we can leave for future generations.

Dear Father, help us to teach our children the importance of the gospel. Help us to review the gospel with them throughout their lives. Help us, dear Lord, to be certain that we put into practice what we learn. Help us to show our children and everyone around us the joy that comes when we live gospel-centered lives. In Jesus' name, Amen.

TIME IS
MOVING ON

September 22, 2010

It all started last year when the AARP Card came in the mail with my name on it. It was the beginning of the cold reality that I have lived for half a century. I remember when I thought fifty was ancient! We now regularly receive mail about retirement plans, retirement villages, and all other things retirement. But the piece of mail that topped it all came this week.

It was from *The Scooter Store*. It begins, "Dear Mr. Jenkins, We've seen it time after time. People who are reluctant to use any mobility assistance because they think they will become dependent on it... That's why we've enclosed a FREE Personal Mobility Assessment... You can't imagine how much a power chair or scooter will add to your well-being, independence, and happiness."

The following types of questions were asked:

- Do you sometimes feel left out by not being able to get together with family and friends?

- Do you have health-related issues that limit your mobility?

- Are you feeling like a bother to others due to limited mobility?

• Have you fallen in the past twelve months?

This all reminds me of a story that V. P. Black related to me one time. He said he had been invited to preach in a special meeting by a church in the northern part of the country. He said to a man he was talking with, "I will be glad to do that, but you all need to know that I am getting older, and I can't get around as easily as I used to." Brother Black told me that he had to make a couple of connecting flights from Alabama to get there, and that at each stop, as well as when he arrived at the final destination, they had a wheelchair waiting for him! Brother Black said, "I may be getting older, but I'm not dead, yet!"

In the chapter, titled "Time's Thief" from his book, *Undone by Easter*, William Willimon relates the account of horror novelist Stephen King being out for a jog one morning when he was hit by a speeding van. King spent weeks in the hospital, "fighting for his life, in terrible pain." In one interview, King admitted that the accident "changed his life, and afterward, he had written some his best novels." King continued, "Still, if someone had given me the choice of retiring peacefully to New England, or getting hit by a van and writing two or three more good books, I would have chosen retirement in a heartbeat." Willimon said, "Listening to that interview, I muttered, 'In my religion, that speeding, disrupting, homicidal van is sometimes named "God."'"

While we may not agree with this theology completely, the point is well made. Our timetable and God's timetable for us are not always the same. We make plans for our lives, and something happens to interrupt those plans. We schedule events, and those schedules are changed.

Many of us live by the clock and the calendar. If our iPhone or computer dies, we are sunk. Willimon makes a wonderful point when he says, "The invention and ubiquity of the clock in modernity gives the illusion of time's uniformity, measurability, and linear progression. The clock makes time fleeting, incessant, and ultimately irretrievable. In modernity, we're always losing time, killing time, and wasting time because we've lost the means to retrieve time past or live into the future. Time without God is denuded, impoverished time, time without meaning. Boredom plagues modern people because we've robbed time of any agency other than our own actions, producing lots of empty boring time with few surprises."

But praise God; he has taken time for us. He took time to create us in his image (Gen. 1:26–27). He took time before he created anything to plan our redemption (Eph. 1:4–6; 3:9–12). God took time to come to this earth through his Son and reveal to us grace and truth (John 1:14). He took time to save us from our sins through the death of his only Son (John 3:16; Rom. 5:8). God took time to give us his Word, a plan that can guide us, comfort us, and teach us how to live (Psa. 119:15). Add to all of this God's faithfulness to man, "Your faithfulness endures to all generations" (Psa. 119:90).

This last verse reminds us that God is not someone who was present only in the past; he is still with us today. Many people want to study God as if he was only active in the past, but our God is still faithful and still loves us, provides for us, cares for us, and answers our prayers in the present!

The times of our lives are bounded by death. We are born, we live a certain number of years, and then we die. Our time here on this earth is restricted. We are limited to what we can accomplish in this life. It is this reality that causes us to want so badly to control our time. We long to have some time back, to change how we've lived in time. We make statements such as, "If I could have just a few more minutes to speak with my mom again, I would tell her how much I appreciated all she did for me during her life. I would tell her how sorry I am for the times I disappointed her and how much I love her." "If I could just spend one more day with my children, I'd talk to them one more time about what I feel is most important for their life. I'd talk with them more about Jesus, about my own weaknesses, and about how important it is to spend time with God. I would tell them how much I love them, and how thankful I am that God brought them into my life."

But we know it can't happen that way because that time is gone. However, this seemingly bad news reveals the best news of all. Even though our lives on this earth are bounded by death, Jesus has defeated death through his resurrection (1 Cor. 15:23–28)! And in defeating death, he defeats the idea of limited time. He gives us eternity. Where time shall be no more, we will never be rushed again, and we will never long to have time back.

One of the blessings of getting older is that we grow to appreciate more the precious moments of time we have with those we love. We realize that there are some things in life that do not matter quite as much as we once believed. We become more willing to speak with people around us about eternity. We know that our time on this earth is brief, and we long for the time when we will be with our Savior (Phil. 3:20–21).

For now, I'll hold off on ordering that scooter. Even though time is moving on, there is still time left, and there is so much that needs to be done. There are too many good times to have, and too many hours that need to be spent encouraging, as well as reaching out to others.

Dear Father, thank you for taking time for us. Thank you for giving us time as a gift, and thank you most of all for defeating the great boundary of time by allowing Jesus to conquer death through his resurrection. Help us, dear God, to use the time we have here to live for You. Help us not to waste time, but to spend our time in sharing the marvelous love of Jesus with others by the things we say and the things we do. Help us to use every moment of time we have to bring glory to you. In Jesus' name, Amen.

WHO'S THE
AUDIENCE?

The question is not, "Should we worship?" We will all worship something or someone. Some worship their cars, their jobs, their families, their friends, their things, or their money. Some have correctly chosen to worship God. The Bible teaches that he *desires* our worship, and that he *deserves* our worship. However, there are numerous questions about the meaning of worship and the methods of worship.

In recent years, the tension surrounding worship has been labeled, "worship wars." Some have suggested that if we want to grow and reach out to non-Christians, our worship must focus on those who attend. This concept has caused some church leaders to ask people in the community what they want out of worship. Even among the people of God, elderships have surveyed the congregation, asking what should be done to enhance the worship experience. Preachers and elders have flocked to large community churches to learn how to "do church."

New ways of worship are becoming more prevalent in churches today. This fairly recent shift in worship services occurred when the goal became to attract the world to the church by making the worship of the church as much like the world as possible. Strangely enough, the one question that should be asked, but is most often omitted in our "worship war" discussions, is the question of "What does God want?" Shouldn't we always seek God's desire first? Rather than looking around at the world, the church should always be looking up to God.

Fortunately for us, there is help in answering the question, "Who's the Audience?" We do not have to speculate, look at the world around us, survey the neighborhood or the members of the church. All we have to do is open God's Word. In the book of Revelation, our brother John was allowed to get a glimpse of worship in heaven. This is an amazing passage of Scripture. In it, we see a great worship service that is in progress in heaven. In the very throne room of God, we get a sense of the majesty and the glory of this worship service. Everything about the worship in heaven makes it clear that all worship should be focused on God.

We learn first that it is worship that honors God. In Rev. 4:2, we read, "At once I was in the Spirit, and behold, a throne stood in heaven, with one seated on the throne." The first thing that John notices is that there is an occupied throne in heaven. This throne represents the absolute authority of God on the earth. John is given a clear picture of a high view of God. This throne is permanent, it is unchanging, and it is unswayed by human leaders and human events. Caesars, presidents, and world leaders come and go. But the throne in Heaven towers over all circumstances of the earth.

The second fact that we learn about worship in heaven is that there is a reverential fear of God. "From the throne came flashes of lightning, and rumblings and peals of thunder, and before the throne were burning seven torches of fire, which are the seven spirits of God" (Rev. 4:5). This totally controls John's attention and reflects the awesome power of the Almighty.

The final element of the worship of heaven is a constant focus on God. Every eye intersects at the throne. Every worshipper has his gaze fixed on God. Verse 10 shows that they are all falling before God and casting their crowns before him. In verse 11, they are continually calling out, "Worthy, worthy, worthy, are you." This should be our cry each time we gather together as God's people. We are to acknowledge the supreme and sovereign will of God. It takes discipline in our lives and hearts to move away from sloppy worship that trivializes our Almighty God. True worship requires much of us. It requires that we prepare our hearts, that we lay aside our selfish desires, that we quit acting like children who seek to be entertained, and that we come with open hearts, open ears, and open eyes ready to exalt the Father, as well as his Son.

Dear God, we give thanks to you for the privilege of worship. Help us to grow in our love for worship and in our understanding of worship. Help us, Lord, to remember that worship is not about us. May we focus all of our energy and our heart on you as we worship. In Jesus' name, Amen.

REMEMBER
& FORGET

September 14, 2012

Sunday, you will stand in front of an audience of people to proclaim the Word of God. In that audience, there will be a someone who is in more physical pain than you can imagine.

In your audience, someone will be contemplating divorce, or hurting because of physical, mental, or social abuse. Someone in your audience will be wondering how they are going to pay their bills this week. Someone will be afraid they are going to lose their job.

In your audience, there will be a teenager who feels guilty because of something they did wrong over the weekend. Someone will be struggling with their prayer life. Someone will wonder if anyone will speak to them today.

In your audience will be someone who has recently lost the closest person in the world to them. Someone will be thinking about the report they are waiting on from the doctor. Someone will be praying that God will help them figure out their future.

In your audience will be a single Christian wondering if they will ever find that special, forever person. Someone will be wondering what happened to that person who promised to care for them forever, but now doesn't seem to care.

In your audience will be children who are not secure because their parents are always fighting. Someone will be consumed with guilt and will be wondering if God will ever love them again.

In your audience, someone will be considering walking away from the Lord and his church. Someone will be waiting for you to tell them what they need to do with their life. Someone will be contemplating giving their life to the Lord.

How in the world can those of us who preach the Word of God navigate this terrain? It might help if we would try to forget a few things and remember a few things.

Just for today, try to forget about the person who told you on the way out the door last week that you mispronounced a word, misquoted a verse, or missed a point on your handout.

Just for today, try to forget about the one elder who has made it clear he wants you gone.

Just for today, try to forget about the failure you had last week.

Just for today, try to forget about the feeling you had because last week's sermon didn't go as planned.

Just for today, try to forget about the repairs that need to be made on your house or car.

Just for today, try to forget about your financial worries.

Just for today, try to forget about that counseling session that has been burdening your heart.

Today, try to remember that you are a man of God (1 Tim. 6:11; 2 Tim. 3:16–17).

Today, try to remember that Jesus is also in your audience, and that he mediates even for you (1 Tim. 2:5).

Today, try to remember that you have the Spirit of God dwelling in you (Rom. 8:9).

Today, try to remember that God has given you a very serious charge (2 Tim. 4:1–4).

Today, try to remember that God will be with you as you proclaim his Word (Deut. 31:6).

Today, try to remember, to boldly approach the throne of God before you preach (Heb. 4:14–16).

Today, try to remember to proclaim the whole counsel of God (Acts 20:27).

Today, try to remember to preach the truth in love (Eph. 4:15).

Today, try to remember to have the mind of Christ as you speak (Phil. 2:5).

Today, try to remember to look at the people with the compassion of Jesus (Matt. 9:36).

Today, try to remember that God loves you unconditionally (John 3:16; Rom. 5:8).

Today, try to remember that you are preaching a transforming message that is Good News (Rom. 1:16).

Today, try to remember that you are a part of a multitude of men who are linked together in the greatest work in the world.

Dear Father, be with those of us who will be proclaiming your Word on Sunday. Help us to remain focused on our task. Help us to never forget that we are preaching a life-changing message. Help us to take those who hear us to the cross. Help us, dear God, to get out of the way so that everyone present can see Jesus. In his name, Amen.

BE CAREFUL, LITTLE MOUTH

December 7, 2011

One of the many aspects about life in Texas that I have grown to love is high school football. There are a number of world-class players each year, and the stadiums look like college stadiums in other parts of the country. I recently had the privilege of going to a high school playoff game with a few friends and watched some of the states top teams. The game turned out to be a blowout.

Though we didn't "have a dog in the fight," we happened to be sitting on the winning team's side. There was the usual yelling and good-natured cheering from the fans. We happened to be sitting just below a couple of really loud guys who were either former players from a few years back, or were frustrated armchair quarterbacks! Throughout the entire game, they yelled at the players, but mostly the coaches. They announced to the crowd before every play what the coach should call, and after the play, why the coach made the wrong call. When the coach called a pass, they droned on about why he shouldn't pass, and then when a pass play worked, they were quieted for a brief moment. When he called a run up the gut, they yelled that he should run outside. It became rather humorous and bothersome at the same time.

The humor was in the fact that they were certain they knew

more than the coach. I know most fans are like this. I've done plenty of Monday morning coaching myself. After all, I played a few years of high school football myself. I feel sure I could have played for the legendary Bear Bryant if he would have just given me a fair chance!

The bothersome part was that they were so vocally critical of some of the players. I thought about the parents, family members, and friends who were in range of their constant berating. I hurt for them if they were able to hear what the "experts" were saying.

This ugly scene reminds me of what I have seen and heard too many times from people in the church. The people who are supposed to bear the image of Jesus can sometimes be so cruel.

I thought about Christians who have spoken unkindly to elders, preachers, and their family members. You know the kind of statements: "Our former preacher would have never said something like that." "The elders in our former congregation would have never made that kind of decision."

I thought about elders who have called the preacher "on the carpet" and read him the riot act because of something they heard from a member without even getting his side of the story.

I thought about preachers who have been publicly critical of elders without considering their wisdom and years of experience.

I thought about church members who have criticized a young family for not "taking care of their children" the way they should have, without ever considering the time, effort, and energy it took to get them ready for Bible study or worship.

I thought about Christians who have jumped on some visitor about the way they dress or behave with no thought that maybe this individual who is seeking God has never been taught anything about worship.

I thought about Christians I know who have convinced themselves that gossiping about others is a "spiritual gift," and it is their duty to tell everything they know.

I thought about Christians who make cruel statements to their spouses that they wouldn't even think about making to anyone else.

I thought about Christian parents who have made statements to their children that have left lasting scars on those children.

I thought about the hurtful words that have been spoken by those who are commanded to let their lights shine before others.

"Let your speech always be gracious, seasoned with salt, so that you may know how you ought to answer each person" (Col. 4:6).

"Let no corrupting talk come out of your mouths, but only such as is good for building up, as fits the occasion, that it may give grace to those who hear" (Eph. 4:29).

Dear Father in heaven, please help us to be people who are careful about the words we allow to come out of our mouths. Help us, Lord, to consider that our words can be both hurtful and helpful. Help us to speak only words that will edify those who hear us. Help us to remember that we should glorify you with everything we say and do. In Jesus' name, Amen.

VICTORIOUS FAITH

March 26, 2012

We understand that faith is one of the key ingredients to our Christian walk. We must have faith if we want to please God (Heb. 11:6). There are times in life when it is relatively easy to have a strong faith. It is easy to have faith when you've just received a clean bill of health from the doctor, or when you've been successful in business. It's easy to have faith when your team has just won a big game, or when you've just aced a big test and you're doing well in school. It's easy to have faith when your marriage is strong and your children are living the way you've taught them. It's easy to have faith when you've preached a sermon that everyone has responded positively toward, and the elders have given you a vote of confidence. It's easy to have faith when you've been victorious over Satan, and you've been able to say no to sin. It's easy to have faith when you're on the mountaintop with Jesus, Moses, and Elijah and you've heard the voice of God (Mark 9:2–7).

But there are many times in our lives that faith is not so easy, when doubts arise—when we question both the Lord and our faith. It's difficult to have faith when the doctor informs you that the tests results were not good, and you don't feel well. It's difficult to have faith when things are not going well at work, and you wonder if you are going to keep your job. It's hard to have faith if your team loses the game, or you don't pass the test in school. It's easy to allow doubts to creep in when your marriage is on the rocks, or when your children have turned away from what you've spent a lifetime teaching them about the Lord. It's easy to doubt when feel like your sermons are dry, when people don't respond well, when the elders question your work, and when it seems things are not going well at church. It's easy to doubt when you've fallen to a particular temptation, and you've said yes to sin. It's easy to have doubts when you come down off the mountain, and you're in the valley where everything seems to be falling apart.

It's important to understand the setting of Mark 9. In the beginning of the chapter, some of the apostles were on the mountaintop with Jesus. While they are standing there, Moses and Elijah appeared. The apostles heard the conversation of Jesus, Moses, and Elijah. Besides this, they heard the voice of God from heaven. Could there be a more perfect picture?

Later in the chapter, they came down from the mountaintop back into the normal routine of life. The first thing they saw when they came down from the mountain was a large crowd and people arguing (Mark 9:14). The first thought in my mind is that it is easier to hear the voice of God when you're on the mountaintop alone than it is when you are in a large crowd of people who are arguing.

A man brought his son to Jesus to heal him. The disciples of Jesus could not heal him, and Jesus described them as an unbelieving generation (Mark 9:19). Jesus healed the boy, and later, the disciples of Jesus questioned their inability to be able to heal him (Mark 9:28). Doubts had entered their minds, they needed an answer from the Lord, and they received a powerful reminder from Jesus. "This kind cannot be driven out by anything but prayer" (Mark 9:29). Prayer can help restore our faith in the Lord by removing the doubts from our minds and hearts. Prayer is a powerful resource that can help us have a victorious faith. Notice also that:

Prayer can reveal the power of God in our life. Facing difficult circumstances is one of the biggest reasons why we often doubt God. Sometimes, doubt is our first response to tough times. Maybe we are dealing with a sickness, or we have just lost a loved one, or maybe we have a marriage that is falling apart, or something that was very important that we lost, or we are struggling in our finances. We are having trouble at work. Things are not going well in our work with the church.

Those difficult circumstances surround us and doubt creeps in. We begin to think—God where are you? God, why would you allow this to happen to me? God, do you really love me? When we pray, we are reminded of God's great promises. We remember that all things work for good for those who love the Lord (Rom. 8:28), that we can do anything through him who gives us strength (Phil. 4:13). Prayer brings faith, and victorious faith removes doubt. Jesus said, "All things are possible for one who believes" (Mark 9:23).

Prayer enables us to look beyond our doubts and see Jesus. One of the problems with doubt is that it often clouds our view. We have a difficult time seeing the Lord. It is possible that one of the reasons for the argument in Mark 9 was the inability of Jesus' disciples to heal the man's son. Perhaps the man began to think that, if the disciples of Jesus couldn't heal him, then Jesus himself couldn't heal him. He did ask Jesus to help his "unbelief" (Mark 9:24). When we have doubts in our mind, unbelief can be just around the corner.

Prayer will refocus our lives on Jesus. It will help erase the doubts and restore the victorious faith we require to navigate the storms of life. If we are going to be able to run the race with endurance," we desperately need to fix our eyes on Jesus, "the author and finisher of our faith" (Heb. 12:1–2 NKJV).

Prayer reminds us of God's plan for our life. All of us are in a constant battle with sin. Satan wants to devour us (1 Pet. 5:8). We often struggle with doing what we know is right vs. not doing what we know is wrong (Rom. 7:15-20). When we struggle in this way, we begin to doubt our faith, and we even begin to doubt God. When we doubt God, we attempt to take things into our own hands.

The disciples of Jesus apparently begin to doubt the plan of the Lord in Mark 9. They wondered out loud why they could not cast the demon out of the man's son. Jesus reminded them of the plan of God, that if they were going to do the work of God, they must pray (Mark 9:29).

We cannot accomplish the work God has planned for us apart from prayer. We cannot live the life God wants us to live without prayer. When we struggle with our health, in our families, with our jobs, and even in the work of the Lord, prayer is our greatest resource.

God has promised us that we can come before his throne at any time (Heb. 4:14–16). Approaching his throne through our High Priest will renew our strength, restore our faith in the Lord's plan, and revive our hearts to live with victorious faith!

Dear Father, help us to live with victorious faith. Help us to see the need for prayer when doubts enter our hearts. Help us, dear God, to pray more often and more fervently. Father, forgive us when we allow doubts to cause us to question your power or your plan. Thank you, dear Lord, for allowing us to come to pray to you at any time. In Jesus' name, Amen.

BE A
BLESSING

February 13, 2013

Recently, while I was feeling under the weather, Laura drove through Chick-fil-A to grab us a bite to eat (is there anything Chick-fil-A cannot cure?). When she drove up to the window after placing her order, the cashier said, "Your meal was paid for by the person in front of you!" Laura said, "Well that was very kind. I'll pay for the meal of the person behind me." The cashier said, "You make the seventh person in a row to buy the meal of the next person in line!"

That seems to me like the definition of paying it forward. We have no idea how many cars after Laura did the same thing. What we do know is that when you bless someone's life, it can become contagious.

On another occasion recently, we were eating at Chili's with a friend of ours who was visiting from out of town. We saw a family from church and went over to their table to visit for a minute. They were delightful. When we were ready to leave after our meal, the waiter said, "That family sitting across from you paid for your meal!" We were overwhelmed with gratitude.

This isn't about money and free meals, but about blessing the lives of others. Think for a minute about all that is accomplished when we bless someone's life.

When we bless others, we are following the example of Christ.

It was said of our Lord, "For even the Son of Man came not to be served but to serve, and to give his life as a ransom for many" (Mark 10:45). Everywhere Jesus went, he was in the blessing business. He blessed the lives of the rich and poor, of the big and small, of the educated and uneducated. Jesus blessed the lives of everyone he met.

When we bless others, we bring joy to their lives. Random acts of kindness will bring great joy to those who receive the blessing. Give it a try. Send a note of encouragement, buy someone a meal, make a visit or a phone call. What you will quickly find is that it doesn't just bring joy to the life of the recipient of the blessing; it also brings great joy to the giver. No wonder Jesus said, "It is more blessed to give than to receive" (Acts 20:35).

When we bless others, we cause others to want to be a blessing. As we said in the beginning of this article, being a blessing to others can be contagious. Someone had to pay the first person's meal in that line at Chick-fil-A. Once that first person stepped out and performed an act of blessing, it started a chain reaction that went on for who knows how long. When you bless someone's life, you might just turn a life around and cause others to be a blessing.

When we bless others, we share the image of Christ. By blessing the lives of others, we show them Jesus. It is our duty to strive to develop the mind of Christ (Phil. 2:5). We have been called to let our lights shine before men so that they might glorify God (Matt. 5:14–16).

Our world is filled with people who take from others, who perform acts of injustice, who are cruel, unkind, and uncaring. What our world desperately needs is to see people who will bless lives, people who will be more like Jesus.

Dear Father, help us to do everything we possibly can to bless the lives of those around us. Help us to show Jesus to the people we meet. Help us, dear God, to bless others through our actions and attitudes. In Jesus' name, Amen.

WE'RE NOT
FOURTH GRADERS

January 20, 2012

Russ and I had breakfast together a couple of days this week. Russ is one of my oldest friends. He and his wife, Linda, come to Texas every January to visit with us for a few days. Russ heads to Lubbock to speak for the Sunset workshop and the girls go shopping.

Russ told me about recently volunteering to help Linda with her first grade Bible class on a Wednesday night. It was a singing night for the adults; therefore, Russ thought it would be a good opportunity for him to spend some time with the children. He decided to talk to them about faith. Russ was waxing eloquently about faith, discussing Scriptures, and even writing notes on the board. He felt pretty good about what he was doing until one of the first grade boys raised his hand and said, "Mr. Russ, we're not fourth graders."

Laura and I recently had the privilege of beginning a Bible study with a young lady who was raised in a foreign country. Until recently, she had never attended a church of Christ, and she knows very little (if anything) about the Bible.

This wonderful young lady, her husband, and their son started visiting our congregation because of an invitation from some co-workers. She has a burning desire to learn more. It is refreshing and challenging to study the Word of God with this couple. Russ's experience in the first grade Bible class, and our experience in this Bible study, have brought me face to face with reality.

Not everyone has the same amount of Bible knowledge. Not everyone was raised in the church. Not everyone has had an opportunity yet to become like those noble Bereans. There are many people who do not understand our religious jargon, and we need to find a language that others can understand.

Begin with people where they are. This makes it paramount that we learn all we can about the religious background and understanding of those with whom we study. Many people are shackled by religious confusion, yet others have no real knowledge of religion at all.

Find common ground. For some, it might be a love for God or Jesus. It might be that others are curious about the church. Some have experienced a loss or some other life difficulty. Surely we can find something in the heart and life of every person that will help us reach them with the Good News.

Spend time before the Father's throne. We need to ask our Lord to help us with our inadequacies (Heb. 4:14–16). If we ever get to the point that we think we know how to handle every question or situation, we are in deep trouble. I desperately need God's help in this particular study.

Don't be afraid to say, "I don't know." I vividly remember my dad saying that when we are studying the Word of God with people, we should never be afraid to say, "I don't know." If a question is raised that we can't answer, it's better to say, "I don't know," than to give a wrong answer. We should tell the person we are studying with that we would have an answer next time we meet. This quality also keeps us from appearing as if we have all knowledge.

Study, study, study. Taking the above suggestion to an extreme could be a crutch that would keep us from studying. We need to do our best to be able to answer questions that might arise (1 Pet. 3:15). This is another reason to spend time getting to know those with whom we study.

Remember that the Lord is with us. There is no one who wants the whole world to know the gospel more than the One who authored it (2 Pet. 3:9). God will do everything possible to help us as we share his Word with others.

May God help those of us who are endeavoring to preach and teach his Word to do our very best for him. Teaching others the Good News about Jesus is the greatest gift we can give to anyone (2 Cor. 9:15). It is a life-changing experience for the one teaching, as well as the one being taught!

Dear Father, help us to be busy sharing the Good News with everyone we can. Help us, God, to remember that not everyone is in the same place. Help us to be aware and to care deeply about those around us. Thank you for bringing people who need to know about Jesus into our lives. May we be instruments of your love, power, and forgiveness. In Jesus' name, Amen.

IT'S NORMAL
TO HURT

December 1, 2011

The holidays are supposed to make us think of words like *thankful*, *merry*, and *happy*. We are supposed to enjoy this time of year. But what if a loved one is not coming home for the holidays? What if this is going to be your first Christmas without your spouse, parent, or your child? What if death, divorce, distance, or decisions causes you to associate the holidays with depression, anxiety, and stress?

Some who are reading this will want to stop right now because you already feel that sharp pain caused by your loss. I would say to you, "Please don't." Some of you are saying, "Jeff, quit being a downer, I love the holidays." I would say to you that I don't want to diminish your joy. However, this is for people who are wondering if it is normal to hurt. If you don't need this, chances are you know someone who does.

The experience of joy during the holidays is not universal. It is not that those who hurt want to be killjoys. If you find yourself in a less than festive attitude right now, I want you to know that it is okay. It is normal to hurt. As a matter of fact, Jesus gives us permission to hurt. He understands. He said to those close to him who were hurting, "I have said these things to you, that in me you may have peace. In the world you will have tribulation. But take heart; I have overcome the world" (John 16:33).

In this passages, Jesus not only tells us that it is normal to experience hurt in this life, giving us permission to hurt, but he also gives us permission to hope! One of the reasons for hope is seeing that our Lord hurt. He knows what it is like to be deeply moved when you lose someone dear to you (John 11:33). He knows what it is like to weep when we lose someone close to us (John 11:35). Jesus knows what it is like to be alone (Matt. 27:46). Through his experiences, he teaches us that it is normal to hurt. And the fact that he endured and overcame gives us reason to hope.

Having endured loss during the holidays, and having spoken with many others who also have experienced loss, please allow me to share a few practical suggestions that might be of help.

Prepare. If you have lost someone close, you know that your emotions can ambush you at any time. If we can attempt to identify just some of those times, we might be able to prepare as those times arrive.

Accept. It might help to accept the difficulty of this time of year. Our losses are real, and the holidays have a tendency to magnify those losses. Remember this is a season—it will pass, and we can continue our journey toward overcoming loss again.

Socialize. Try not to hibernate during the holidays. The overwhelming feelings you have may tempt you to isolate yourself. But try to force yourself to be with others. Make sure it is people you enjoy spending time with.

Lower your expectations just a little. Remember that many Christmas songs and movies paint an unrealistic picture of the holidays. Not everything is as it appears on the TV screen. Do your best to listen to songs and watch programs that bring you joy.

Don't anesthetize. Many people try to numb the pain of the holidays with drugs or alcohol. It is a fact that trying to numb emotional distress with chemicals can create even more depression and pain.

Reconsider. It might help to rethink how you decorate during the holidays. If old ornaments or decorations cause too much pain, don't display them this year. It's OK to set them aside for another time. One friend told of how they didn't even celebrate Christmas in their home for a few years after losing their son. They went to a different location.

Take care of yourself. Take care of your physical, emotional, and spiritual well-being. Exercise whenever you can. Spend time with people who bring you joy. Above all, spend time in prayer and worship with your Father in heaven.

Don't force yourself. If going to the mall and being around a million people is too stressful, consider shopping online. It's an easy way to stay out of the chaos of busy stores.

Develop. Work on some coping strategies. Keep the phone number of a close friend, your elders, your preacher, or a counselor nearby. Make a commitment to yourself that, if you feel negative thoughts taking over, you will call someone. There are people who would love to help.

Turn on the lights. Get as much sunshine as possible. Winter has a way of taking its toll on our emotions by the loss of daylight. Studies have proven that many of us are Vitamin D deficient. It's okay to take a Vitamin D supplement, but we also need to be in the daylight when we can.

Set boundaries. Communicate specifically to family and friends what you are capable of doing during this time of year, and what you are not capable of doing. Don't let others make you feel guilty or force you into taking on more than you can handle.

Reach out. Find others who might be alone during the holidays and reach out to them. Do something for someone else. It has been my experience that when I am down, if I will do something for someone else, it always makes me feel better.

Pray. Ask God to help you to be strong during the holidays. Ask him to surround you with people who will bring you joy. Ask your Father to help you find hope in the midst of your hurt (2 Cor. 1:3–7).

My prayer is that these thoughts will be of some help to those who are hurting. Above all things, remember that it's normal to hurt, and there is hope to be found in Jesus.

Dear Father in heaven, today we pray for those who are hurting during the holidays. Our prayer is that they may know of your great love, comfort, and concern. Help us to encourage one another. Dear God, help us to be sensitive to the pain of those around us. We are thankful for your love for us in sending Jesus into the world. We are thankful that he taught us that it is normal to hurt, and that he continues to give us hope. In Jesus' name, Amen.

A HEART THAT SEEKS THE LORD

October 17, 2012

He is almost ninety years of age. He called to see if he could visit with me for just a few minutes after Wednesday night Bible study. My dear brother said, "You've probably noticed that I've missed a few services lately?" He explained how his wife has not been feeling well. A few times recently, she had asked him to stay home with her because she didn't want to be by herself while sick. He said he wished he could be here every time we meet.

With tears in his eyes, the brother said to me, "I have prayed about this, and I am doing what I think is right, but I just wanted you to know." We prayed together, and I expressed my appreciation to him for letting me know. I also told him that, if it mattered, I believed he was doing the right thing.

After he left my office, I prayed again. My prayer this time was that God would help me to never make such a person feel bad for taking care of their spouse. Additionally, my prayer was that God would raise up more men like this brother for the church.

Compare the attitude, the desire, and the heart of this dear brother:

- To Christians who say, "I have to work hard and need to rest instead of coming to church on Wednesday night or Sunday night."

- To Christians who say, "I don't really like the class choices or the teachers, so I am going to stay home."

- To Christians who say, "I am protesting against the leadership because I disagree with their decisions."

- To Christians who say, "I'm not happy with the direction of the church, I don't like the songs, or I don't agree with the way the worship services or classes are conducted."

- To Christians who say, "I'm angry because not very many people speak to me."

- To Christians who say, "I don't think the church does enough in the community."

This is not meant to make those with legitimate reasons for missing church feel guilty. Some who read this will be offended and some will disagree. It is not my intention to offend. However, some of the above mentioned "reasons" for missing worship and times of study are just plain selfish.

- What about being present because you want to encourage your brothers and sisters in the Lord (Heb. 10:24)?

- What about being present because you want to grow spiritually through the study of the Word of God (1 Pet. 2:2)?

- What about being present because you want to grow closer to other Christians?

- What about being present because you want to teach young people what it means to have a closer walk with the Lord?

- What about being present because you love the Lord with all of your heart, soul, mind, and strength?

- What about being present because you want to put the Lord first in every aspect of your life (Matt. 6:33)?

- What about being present because you don't want to forsake the assembly of the saints (Heb. 10:25)?

- What about being present because you love to be involved in fellowship with other Christians?

- What about being present because you are an important part of the Body of Christ and you are needed?

Dear Father, please help us think seriously about the need for being present when the church meets. Help us to put your desires over our own. Help us dear God, to think about how our decisions affect others. Thank you, Father, for the wonderful example and influence of those who teach us how to live. In Jesus' name, Amen.

CONSISTENT LIVES

April 5, 2012

L ast week, Laura and I flew to Tennessee where I was speaking for a lectureship. On the plane, I caught up on a few emails and was going over my thoughts for the lesson to be presented about family. Laura was looking through the airlines magazine, and a story caught her eye. It was about five individuals who formed a bond when they met because they were all Road Warriors. They were named this year's top Road Warriors by the airline.

A Road Warrior, according to the story, is a person who understands the "difficulty of being away from home for days, weeks, or even months at a time." In addition, they understand what it means to deal with "last-minute or unexpected travel changes."

The article contained a short bio of each individual, then a number of questions that each of them were asked during the interview. You know the kind of questions that are asked in this type situation:

- What was the defining moment in your career?
- What is your favorite meal?
- If you could take a vacation anywhere in the world, where would it be?

- What was the last item you purchased?

- What is the one piece of technology you can't live without?

- What was the last song you heard?

- What do you do when you need inspiration?

- If you could meet anyone (dead or alive), who would it be, and why?

Great questions for any group that wants to get to know each other. Sounds a little similar to some of the questions that we've attempted to answer with a group of friends on a road trip or at dinner. The most interesting interview was the Second-Prize Winner—a jovial looking fellow who obviously has a zest for life. When asked whom he would most like to meet, he responded by saying, "Jesus Christ." His favorite meal? Barbecued chicken and beer! When asked what he does when he needs inspiration, he said, "I drink beer!" His seemingly convoluted answers caused me to think. Is it possible for someone to have a strong admiration and interest in Jesus while at the same time live a rather immoral life?

Can people have a divided heart and mind? Then I remembered the words that Jesus quoted from the prophet Isaiah, "This people honors me with their lips, but their heart is far from me" (Matt. 15:8). In addition, there are numerous examples of people in Scripture who at one moment seemed to love God with all of their hearts, but the next moment they were caught up in sin. The man after God's own heart (1 Sam. 13:14; Acts 13:22) says in one prayer to God, "I have stored up your word in my heart, that I might not sin against you" (Psa. 119:11), and in another prayer he asks for God's forgiveness for committing adultery and murder (Psalm 51:1–4)!

So what does all this mean to us? It means anyone can fall. It means we all need the kind of forgiveness offered because of Jesus. It means that those of us who claim to have a great love for and allegiance to Jesus need to constantly examine our hearts (2 Cor. 13:5). It means we should continually encourage one another and build each other up (1 Thess. 5:11). We need to challenge one another to remain strong, and when one of us falls, we need to be there to help each other.

When we fall, we need to be willing to ask for forgiveness from the Father and from one another. We need to be forgiving toward one another so that we can be more like our Father (Matt. 6:14–15). We need to live more consistent lives so that we can be more like Jesus.

Father, we thank you for being the God of the second chance. We thank you for loving us even when we were unlovable. Thank you, dear God, for sending Jesus to die for us even while we were sinners. Thank you for your forgiveness. Help us, Father, to do our best to be more consistent in the way we live. Help us when we fall to get up and try again. Help us to be more like Jesus. In his name, Amen.

A MODEL FOR MARRIAGE

July 15, 2010

The news about marriage these days is generally not very encouraging. If you look at the news and hear the stories about Mel Gibson, Al Gore, and a host of others, it causes you to wonder if anybody is working to make their marriage strong. If you watch television and movies, you can see that marriage is portrayed in these venues as a joke. Homosexual unions are lauded and portrayed as the norm in the mindless world of many sitcoms.

It has been our privilege through the years to know a few couples that have been married for more than seventy years. The couple we have known the best are Bill and Dorothy. They will never have their name up in lights because most people in our world do not recognize the greatness they exemplify.

I wish every person could get to know this wonderful couple. I wish everyone could hear the story about how they met, about their dating years, their early years of marriage, and their commitment to one another since their wedding on February 4, 1939.

When our family was transitioning from Oklahoma to Texas, Bill and Dorothy invited us to live in their home. We had the privilege of spending many hours with them during those days. They were gracious hosts, whether it was eating at their table, having dessert, playing Rumikub, watching a ball game, watching the family dog perform his many tricks, or just sitting and talking.

Dorothy is a hugger. She has a wonderful, sweet spirit that welcomes everyone. She freely says, "I love you," and she shows it by the way she lives her life. Bill is a delightful man. He has a marvelous sense of humor, his stories are delightful, and his advice is overflowing with wisdom. Through the years, he has written poetry and love letters to Dorothy, as well as lessons that he has shared with his co-workers at the hospital where he volunteers. A couple of years ago, Bill was honored by being named *Volunteer of the Year* at the hospital. He has delivered a few of those lessons at church, and they are always outstanding. At ninety plus years young, Bill still plays golf every week.

Bill and Dorothy are both givers, not takers. They exemplify the spirit of humility. Bill and Dorothy would not want this to be written about them. However, I will run the risk of getting in trouble; in a world that seems to no longer understand marriage, their story needs to be told.

We desperately need to hold up couples like Bill and Dorothy to our young people. They need to know that what they see on TV and in movies is not the only way. They need to know that God has designed a better way and that there are people who have followed God's plan who have been extremely successful. While reflecting upon seventy plus years of marriage, Bill wrote down some thoughts. I wanted to share them with you in the hope that they will bless your marriage, just as Bill and Dorothy have blessed our lives.

Bill has titled his thoughts, "Five Marriage Remarks." Thank you, Bill, for sharing your wisdom. Thank you, Bill and Dorothy, for being a model we can all imitate. Thank you to all of the other godly couples who are showing us the better way.

I want to talk to you about marriage. What a great institution it is, and why not? God organized the first one with Adam and Eve. Lots of people wonder how two people can live together for over seventy years or until death separates them. But that is God's plan— one man for one woman for life! Your contract is for life. You will have lots of ups and downs. You should be willing to carry each other's burdens. Watch your finances. They will cause more separations and heartaches than anything else. But it can be done, and it sure gets sweeter every year!

I want to give you some advice as to what we should say to our mates that might help our marriages. Just five remarks, and we will start with five words for the first remark, and then four words for the next remark, and then on down to one word.

- 5 Words: "I am proud of you." Don't wait for your mate to say it first. This is something we all like to hear, and more than once a week.

- 4 Words: "What do you think?" Anytime there is something big going to happen (e.g. going on vacation, buying a car, or new house—anything that involves the whole family), we should talk about.

- 3 Words: "I love you." This is so important to say. Not only say it, but show it by your actions: with a kiss, a hug, or a surprise gift is always nice. It does not have to be a special occasion, or when you have done something wrong.

- 2 Words: "I'm sorry." This is something we must say a lot, but it must be from the heart. It is alright for your mate to show their hurt by their action.

- 1 Word: "We." Anytime there is something that involves the whole family, it must not be "What shall I do?" but "What shall we do? " The whole family should decide it. You should talk about it and pray about it. Pray,

pray, pray—morning, noon, and night. It is alright for everyone to speak their mind. A marriage with God in control will always work out for the best.

Friends are very important, and your mate should be your BEST friend.

Dear God, we thank you that in your infinite wisdom, you saw the need for marriage. We are thankful for godly couples who teach us how to keep our marriage commitment. Help us to follow their example and help us to follow the marriage manual you have provided for us in your Word. In Jesus' name, Amen.

ENCOURAGE YOUR KIDS TO LOVE GOD

April 21, 2011

S ome time back, my good friend, Neil Richey, asked me to write
an article for a new on-line publication he has started. The title
of my article was, "Daddy, Encourage Your Boys to Preach." The
need for strong Christians is as great in our day as it has ever been
before. The greatest encouragement for our children to live Christian
lives no doubt comes from the home. My goal in this article is to
encourage parents to encourage their children. My prayer is that
these suggestions will be helpful to that end.

Be the spiritual leader of your home. Paul instructed fathers to
bring their children up "in the discipline and instruction of the Lord"
(Eph 6:4). God has always expected fathers to take the leadership in
teaching and training their sons (Deut. 6:1–9). There is no substitute
for a man of God leading the family. Dad, allow your children to hear
you read and pray. Let them see you active in the life of the church.

Surround your children with strong Christians. I remember
as a boy having Gus Nichols, Guy N. Woods, V. P. Black, Jack
Evans, Charles Coil, Thomas B. Warren, and numerous other great
preachers in our home. These men made an indelible impression
upon a young boy's life. I am thankful for a dad who recognized the
need for his sons to meet great men of God. Take your children to

gospel meetings, lectureships, seminars, and other events where they can be exposed to great gospel preaching. Buy them books written by and about great Christians.

Speak positively about the work of the church. If our children hear us bashing the church and speaking negatively about preachers, they will not want to be Christians. We do not have to paint untrue pictures, but we must show our children the good in the Lord, his church, and his preachers.

See that your children have opportunities to learn about the church. Many congregations offer special classes for young men to learn about public service in the church. Programs such as Lads-to-Leaders offer young men excellent opportunities to hone their skills. A growing number of congregations are offering Preacher Training Camps for young men to be associated with other young men who have an interest in preaching and to learn from older preachers. These types of mentoring situations are outstanding ways for us to encourage our children.

Seize the time while they are young. We all know our children are most impressionable during their formative years. While they are young and in our homes may not be the only time that their lives will be shaped, but it may well be the only chance we have to influence them.

Show them how. Take your children with you when you make visits to hospitals, shut-ins, etc. Take them with you when you have Bible studies. This will provide not only excellent teaching opportunities, but it will also provide wonderful bonding time between a father and his children.

Support our children in the decisions they make. Our attitude should be that, as long as they are faithful Christians, we will be proud of them.

Smother them with the love of Christ, regardless of what they choose to do. There are thousands of faithful children of God who are not preachers or elders. Many godly men are businessmen, teachers, coaches, etc. We should show the love and grace of God to our children in whatever they choose to do with their lives. We should not force them to be something they are not, and we should not try to make them only what we want them to be.

Shower your children with prayer. We should pray that our children would grow to be faithful Christian leaders. We should pray that God would give us the discernment to be the right kind of examples for our children. We should pray that God would give our children wisdom to choose the proper influences when they leave home.

Dear Father in heaven, we pray that you would raise up more faithful Christians. Help those of us who have been blessed with children to do our part in raising more faithful children of God. We thank you for giving us precious children who are such a rich blessing to our lives. Help us to show them what it means to love you and serve you. In Jesus' name, Amen.

FIRST
STEP

October 7, 2011

Laura and I had the joy of being with our sweet granddaughter, Evie, on her first birthday last week. Our precious little one-year-old bundle of joy has brought more happiness to us than we could have ever dreamed possible. We love to hold her, watch her, listen to her, and just spend time with her. We thank God for her every day. We also thank God that she is blessed with two wonderful parents. We are proud of them, and we know they will continue to raise her in the way that will please the Lord.

During her birthday party, we watched her as she took her first step! She has taken a few more since then, and we know she'll be walking everywhere soon. We pray that the Lord will allow us to see her take many steps throughout her life.

We pray we will see her take steps in learning. We are thankful that our sweet Evie will grow up in a home where she will learn. Her first party theme was books. She received many books from friends and family. She will be taught to read those books, and she will learn a great deal. She will also learn the truth of God's Word. She will be taught Scripture. She is already learning in Bible classes and from her parents. She will hear God's Word preached, and she will learn how to live a life that pleases him.

We pray we will see her take steps of obedience. Evie will learn to obey her parents. She will be taught to honor her parents, and she will learn to trust their guidance. She will be taught to obey others who are in authority over her. She will be taught to obey the Lord above everyone else. It will be thrilling to watch her take that step into the water where she will obey the Lord's command to be baptized.

We pray we will see her take steps that will lead to good friendships. Our prayer is that she will be surrounded all her life with people who share the same ideas, goals, and dreams that she will hold dear to her heart.

We pray we will see her step down the aisle of marriage. We pray even now that when she takes that first step down the aisle, that the young man who waits for her at the front will be a man of God. We pray that he will have learned from his own parents the importance of being the spiritual leader in the family. We pray that their marriage will be a match made in heaven, and that their home will be filled with great joy. We pray that their home will be centered on Jesus, and that they will grow together each step of the way.

We pray we will see her take steps of service. Our prayer is that our sweet little Evie will learn to serve those around her. We want to see her reach out and show the love of Jesus to those around her. We pray she will follow in the steps of Jesus as she serves others.

That first step in a child's life is exciting and important. However, there are thousands of other steps they will take, and they need guidance from godly parents, grandparents, and friends as they step through life.

Dear Father, we thank you for precious children. We thank you for what they mean to our lives. We thank you for the joy they bring. Help us, Lord, to influence them in powerful ways. Help us to teach them your Word, and help us to live the kind of lives that they will want to follow. In Jesus' name, Amen.

IS SUNDAY SCHOOL A WASTE?

September 3, 2010

Has there ever been a bigger waste than Sunday school?" That was the question raised by one of the guys recently on a sports talk show. The discussion started with how there is, in their opinion, "way too much sports information in the world." The participants were talking about how much they missed the old days when you got Dallas Cowboys news only a couple of times a week and how you could watch *The Tom Landry Show* every Sunday.

One of the guys talked about how he hated church because it often made him miss that show. And he especially hated Sunday school. Then the men involved began to discuss all of the many reasons they hated Sunday school and why, in their words, "It was such a beating."

I began thinking. Is Sunday school a waste? It appears many Christians might agree with what the sports guys had to say. Many Christians choose to never attend Sunday school because it is too early, too long, too boring, or they just don't want to take the time to be there.

It is possible that a church can de-emphasize Sunday school by not putting any emphasis on it at all. When we do not provide quality Bible classes with teachers who show up prepared and on time, we may be saying with our actions that Sunday school is a waste.

If we spend our time talking about current events, bashing other churches that we happen to disagree with in matters of opinion, and a general failure to teach the Word of God, we may be saying that Sunday school is a waste.

When we put little time and effort in making children's classrooms conducive to learning with joy, we may be saying Sunday school is a waste. When teachers give warmed-over lessons and do not make the study of the Word interesting, we may be saying that Sunday school is a waste.

The great Ira North was credited with saying, "As the Sunday school goes, so goes the congregation!" He used it often, but he said he got it from brother C. J. Garner who was a part of the staff at Madison. Brother North felt so strongly about the Sunday school that he dedicated his book, "Balance," to his wife and to all those who attended "Sunday morning Bible school at the Madison church of Christ." With this attitude about Sunday school, the work of many, and the help of God, the Madison church grew to more than 5,000 members, and on several occasions, they had more than 8,000 in attendance at Sunday school! One could argue that in the minds of millions of people around the world, Sunday school is not a waste.

There are some steps we can take as a church and as individual Christians to make sure Sunday school does not become a waste. All of us can help make Sunday school a life-changing event every time we come together.

Understand why Sunday school is important. It is important because much of our spiritual growth depends largely on our knowledge of God's Word (1 Pet. 2:2; 2 Pet. 3:18). When Christians grow spiritually, the church can grow in every way. Another reason Sunday school is so important is because it gives Christians a wonderful opportunity to fellowship with one another and encourage one another (Heb. 10:24).

Promote Sunday school attendance. Every Christian can

encourage others to attend Sunday school by attending themselves. Do you attend Sunday school? Do you think it is important? If you are not attending now you may be saying by your absence, that Sunday school is a waste. Parents should see that their children are in Sunday school and that they attend as well. Elders and preachers should spend more time "talking up" the need for each member to attend Sunday school.

We should provide our teachers with every resource available. Why not make the latest technology available to those who teach our children? If children attend schools where they use the most current technology possible, then come to Sunday school and we offer old, tired methods, will they come to believe Sunday school is important to us? In many cases, we may not be able to afford the most up-to-date technology. If that is the case, we should still put whatever resources we can into showing our children how important we believe Sunday school really is. In addition to this, we should provide opportunities for our teachers to grow in their knowledge of God's Word. We could host teacher-training workshops or send our teachers to workshops in other places.

If God's people have a strong desire to grow in our faith, if we want to build up one another, and if we want to strengthen the church, then we will work hard to show the world that Sunday school is not a waste. Why not make a special effort to be in Sunday school this week? Your presence can help ensure that it will not be a waste.

Dear Father, help us to see the importance of Sunday school in our own lives and in the life of the church. Help us to show our children and those around us that it is vital for us to grow in our knowledge of your Word. Dear God, help us to show them that one way we can accomplish this is through an outstanding Sunday school program. Help us to teach as many people as possible about Christ. In his name, Amen.

YOU BETTER
WATCH OUT

December 20, 2010

When J. Fred Coots and Haven Gillespie penned these words in the early 1930s, I doubt they realized that it would become an annual Christmas classic. I doubt they knew these words would be loved and sung by children around the world for generations to come. The song begins with the words, "You better watch out..." Not just because Santa Claus is coming to town, but because you never know who else is watching.

A couple of weeks ago, Laura had gone up to see our granddaughter in Oklahoma for the weekend, and I decided on Saturday to catch up on a few jobs that I had been putting off. One was to get the oil changed in my car. I don't change my own oil. One reason is because I never seem to find the time. Another reason is because I find coupons that allow me to get it done for about as much as it would cost to do it myself . So I had a really good coupon and called the place to see how long I would have to wait. The guy said, "Bring it on in; there will be no wait." It took me ten minutes to get there, and by the time I arrived, there was a wait! The fellow said, "I can't believe it happened, but right after you called, we got busy! It will be an hour before we can work you in."

I left and decided to check Wal-Mart. I wasn't very happy as I drove into the service area, but tried to keep my composure. I pulled out my coupon, held it out the window, and said, "Do y'all match other company coupons?" The guy said, "Well sure, for you, Jeff, we do!" I honestly didn't recognize this gentleman at first, and then he said, "I'm sorry I haven't been able to visit church lately. They've changed my schedule and have me working every Sunday." I asked him if he could make it to the 6:00 service, and he said he would try. Then he said, "Thanks for always being so kind to me when I attend worship!"

His kindness and attitude quickly transformed my sour mood. And it's a good thing. While waiting for the car, I decided to walk over to Sam's Club to see what kind of snacks they were giving away. While there, I was in a much better mood and ran into four of our outstanding singles from church. They had been to visit one of our elderly members that morning, and now they were getting ready for the singles Christmas party that would take place that night. We had a nice little visit, and I went on my way. I prayed a prayer of thanksgiving that my attitude had changed before running into them.

One of the many reasons we had better watch out is because we never know who is watching us. The apostle Paul instructed us to be an example in the way that we conduct our life (1 Tim. 4:12). Peter added a similar thought in 1 Pet. 2:12: "Keep your conduct among the Gentiles honorable, so that when they speak against you as evildoers, they may see your good deeds and glorify God on the day of visitation." The way we conduct ourselves as children of God, during this season and at every time of the year, can help determine how those around us view God. It can shape how people view the church. It may help determine where someone close to us spends eternity.

Christians should also keep in mind that there is another One who is watching us at all times. The One who created us, who gave us a new life, and who blesses us every day beyond measure. Heb. 4:13 says, "No creature is hidden from his sight, but all are naked and exposed to the eyes of him to whom we must give account."

As you enjoy time with family and loved ones in the coming days, remember who you are, as well as whose you are. Remember that, as a child of God, you are representing Jesus. Be serious about having the mind of Christ (Phil. 2:5), following in his footsteps (1 Pet. 2:21), and allowing him to be formed in you (Gal. 4:19). Keep in mind that someone who looks up to you may be watching how you represent the King.

Dear Father in heaven, help us remember that we are surrounded every day by people who are watching how we live. Help us, dear God, to live in such away that we will help lead others to Jesus and not turn them away from Jesus. Thank you, Father, for allowing Jesus to come into the world to show us how we should live. Help us, dear God, to love those around us with the love of Jesus. In his name, Amen.

IT'S HIS
FAULT

January 13, 2011

She was a kind nurse who was giving me an exam so that I can purchase new life insurance. She had come to my office to administer the exam, and she asked, "So what do you do here at the church?" Of course, I thought about giving her the answer that many of the Lewisville members might give and say, "Nothing." I settled on telling her that I did the preaching.

She responded by saying, "He must be trying to tell me something."

"Who?" I asked.

"God. You are my second preacher to examine in the past week." I thought, "Maybe God is trying to tell us something!"

I asked her if she had a church, and she said not presently. I invited her to come visit with us, and she assured me that she would. She said, "I'll have to sneak out because my husband doesn't want me to go to church." She told me about how he has a terminal illness. I told her I was sorry, and that I would pray for them both. She said, "Well, it's his fault!" Then she explained that to me and she was right. He had been involved in terrible sin, and the consequence of his sin is a life-ending illness. I was reminded of the fact that all death, disease, problems, and heartaches are in this world because of sin.

The sad reality is that we live in a fallen world.

I do not believe that every problem every individual endures is because of personal sin. We sometimes do people a great injustice by claiming that problems occur because of sin when we fail to explain exactly what we mean.

Job's friends tried to convince him that all his problems were a result of his personal sin. Satan is still trying to convince God's people of this today. Remember that he walks on the earth like a roaring lion, trying to devour the people of God (1 Pet. 5:8).

Some problems are the result of personal sin. Suppose an individual gets drunk and drives their car off into a ditch. Their sin (getting drunk) could result in having to be in a hospital, the loss of their car, financial concerns, etc. The biblical teaching on this is found in Gal. 6:7–8. "Do not be deceived: God is not mocked, for whatever one sows, that will he also reap. For the one who sows to his own flesh will from the flesh reap corruption, but the one who sows to the Spirit will from the Spirit reap eternal life."

Some problems are the result of the sins of others. It has been my sad experience to see some wonderful families devastated because of a selfish individual who is a part of the family. A man who can't keep his temper under control beats his wife and children. The children had nothing at all to do with their father's anger, but they receive lifelong physical and emotional scarring.

A grown child brings pain (financial, emotional, etc.) on parents because of lifestyle, financial, or spiritual decisions made because they think they know better than the parents.

A family suffers financial loss because someone has a gambling problem that they refuse to get under control.

A drunk driver loses control of the car and someone else is killed because of the accident. These are just a few of many examples that explain how sometimes we suffer because of the sin of someone else.

Some problems are a result of the fact that sin exists in our world. When Adam and Eve sinned in the Garden of Eden, sin entered the world. It will remain in the world as long as the world exists. Because sin exists, problems result. That is why we don't want to stay in the world forever. That is why we want to spend eternity in heaven. There will be no sin in heaven; therefore, there will be no pain, no heartache, no problems, and no tears (Rev. 21:4).

I have spoken to numerous Christians during my years of preaching who are carrying guilt that they do not have to carry. Too many Christians have been convinced that, if they are suffering, they must have done something wrong. My prayer is that this will help us to see that this is not always the case. As a matter of fact, it is my conviction that God does not punish people directly today. There are certain consequences that occur because of certain sins, but I don't personally believe they are God-inflicted.

As long as we have life, God allows us opportunity to repent of our sin. Once this life is over, God will judge us. If we are found to be guilty, we will receive eternal punishment (Matt. 25:46). But for those who are in Christ, there is no condemnation (Rom. 8:1)!

Dear Father in heaven, we are thankful that you allowed your Son to die for us so that we might be forgiven of sin. We pray that we will not be guilty of bringing pain to others because of our sin. We pray, dear God, that those who have received forgiveness will understand that there is no need for guilt. Help us to always walk in the light of your love, and help us to grow in our faith every day. In Jesus' name, Amen.

STUDYING THE
WORD OF GOD

March 16, 2012

I had lunch the other day with an old preacher. We get together on occasions, and it is always a delightful experience for me. My friend has been a preacher for well over fifty years, and he is still preaching! He is no longer in what we sometimes call "local work," but he still preaches. Whenever we meet, we always talk about our health, our families, our common friends, and the work of the preacher. I love our time together. He makes me glad I am a preacher, and I hope I can grow old(er) like him.

During our conversation today, he told me that he had been reading more lately. He said that along with his normal Bible reading, he has been listening to audiobooks. He said that during his Bible reading, he was finding more sermons than he had found in a long time. He gave me a great idea for a sermon from his reading of Exodus. He also mentioned to me that, as he thought back through the years, everything in his life seemed to go better when he read the Bible more.

That last statement was very enlightening to me. It is a thought that could really only come from someone who has experienced much of life. So studying the Word of God helps us make sense out of life.

We learn about the work of God. Often, Jesus made it clear that he came to earth to do his Father's will. In fact, one of the earliest recorded statements from Jesus was when his earthly parents thought they had lost him. They found him in the temple and questioned him. He responded by saying, "Did you not know that I must be in my Father's house?" (Luke 2:49).

This statement became the theme of our Savior's life. "I seek not my own will but the will of him who sent me" (John 5:30). "For I have come down from heaven, not to do my own will but the will of him who sent me" (John 6:38). Besides this, Jesus connected what he did with the Word of God. "I do nothing on my own authority, but speak just as the Father taught me" (John 8:28). "We must work the works of him who sent me while it is day; night is coming, when no one can work" (John 9:4).

On one occasion, he made the astounding statement, "I always do the things that are pleasing to him" (John 8:29). Our Savior then tells us what that work was all about. "For the Son of Man came to seek and to save the lost" (Luke 19:10). Clearly Jesus understood the work of God because he had received the Word of God. The work of God has never changed. Our task on this earth involves participating in the work of God. The work of God is to do everything possible to bring men to salvation (Matt. 28:18–20; Rom. 1:16; 2 Pet. 3:9).

We receive a wealth of knowledge about life. Peter reminds us that God has given us everything that we need "that pertain to life and godliness" (2 Pet. 1:3). The same apostle tells us that, if we are going to grow in this life, we are to be like babies and we are to "long for the pure spiritual milk" (1 Pet. 2:2). Further, he tells us that we should "grow in the grace and knowledge of our Lord and Savior Jesus Christ" (2 Pet. 3:18). Life is full of questions and uncertainties. For us to navigate this life, we need the very best roadmap possible. Thank God that he has given us his marvelous Word to guide us. David understood this so well when he wrote, "Your word is a lamp to my feet and a light to my path" (Psa. 119:105). As we read the words of Jesus and the words about him, we learn the true meaning of life. We receive direction for life. "I am the way, and the truth, and the life. No one comes to the Father except through me" (John 14:6).

We learn something about the ways of God. While we cannot fully understand the ways of God (Isa. 55:8–9), through his Word, God has revealed what we need to know about his ways.

Through the revealed Word, we learn about the grace of God (John 1:14), the righteousness of God (Rom. 1:17), the wrath of God (Rom. 1:18; Eph. 5:6), the mercy of God (Eph. 2:4; 1 Pet. 2:10), and the love of God (John 3:16; Rom. 5:8).

For these reasons and many others, we should never quit studying our Bibles. We live such busy lives in this fast-paced, temporary home of ours. There seems to always be more to do than we have time to do it. If our life is going to remain somewhat sane, we need to read our Bibles.

Most of us are familiar with the famous quote that has been attributed to Charles Spurgeon and Vance Havner, "A Bible that's falling apart is usually owned by someone who isn't!" Regardless of who said it, in our hurried lives, we need to remember it. I am thankful for my old friend for the example he is to me. I am also thankful for the wonderful reminder he gave me about the importance of studying.

Dear Father, please help us to make time in our busy lives to study your Word. Father, we want to know your Will for our lives, and we want to know everything we can about your ways. Help us, dear God, to understand that you have given us a wealth of valuable knowledge about this life in your Word. Thank you for loving us so much that you have revealed yourself to us through your Word. Father, we want to know you better. Please forgive us for failing to know your Word and help us to do better. In Jesus' name, Amen.

ARE YOU HAPPY ALL THE TIME?

February 25, 2011

It was a chilly Friday morning due to a cold front coming through North Texas the night before. I was on my way to the hospital and decided to stop by the convenience store to grab a hot cup of French Vanilla cappuccino. When I got to the counter to pay, the lady behind the counter said, "Would you like a Kit-Kat?" I said, "No, thank you."

She then said, "How about a banana?" To which I again said, "No, thank you." But she wasn't through with her sales pitch yet.

She said, "Did you know that bananas are good for you, and not just because of the potassium? They also have serotonin, which is released when you eat one, and it makes you feel happy." I said, "I eat a banana most days."

She said, "Do you feel good all the time?" I couldn't lie, so I said, "Not all the time."

She kept going, "Do you feel happy all the time?" I said, "I do most of the time."

She replied, "Good, keep eating bananas!"

As I drove away, my mind was flooded with thoughts based on our brief conversation. I'm not sure if she works for the convenience store or Chiquita. I wasn't aware that convenience store employees could also serve as medical experts. I didn't know the good folks at the convenience store would be so interested in my constant happiness. I had been happy until I pulled in and noticed that the price of gas had gone up again!

It also caused me to think about our lives as Christians. What makes us happy and what makes us sad? Is there a difference between being happy all the time and living a life filled with joy?

First, what about happiness vs. joy? It appears happiness is based primarily on events, circumstances, and can last either a short period of time or a long one. If circumstances are favorable, then you are happy. If circumstances are unfavorable, then you will not be happy. So maybe eating a banana can make you happy.

On the other hand, joy is more a state of the heart. It is more a part of who we are. After all, the Bible does tell us that our lives should be filled with joy. "Rejoice in the Lord always..." (Phil. 3:1; 4:4). While happiness may be fleeting, joy can last a lifetime. Potentially, a person could be unhappy, yet still have joy in their life. Because the kind lady at the convenience store brought up the idea of happiness, it allowed me to focus on that wonderful emotion for a time.

I'm happy when I'm with my wife. Laura and I have been married nearly thirty years. As we grow older, I find that the more I am with her, the happier I am. We love our children, and we enjoyed them as they were growing up, but we are really enjoying our time together now.

I'm happy when I'm with my friends. Through the course of a lifetime, we develop many friends. Some will be short-term friendships that will last through a specific stage of life. Others will last a lifetime. We currently have some friends who are the dearest people on earth to us. We love our time with them. We laugh together, worship together, pray together, cry together, play together, and love life together.

I'm happy with my work. If I could live ten lives, I would not change what I am blessed to do with my life. To be able to proclaim the Word of God each week to people who love the Lord is the greatest blessing in life. To be able to see lives transformed through the teaching of the Word and the ministry of the church is a tremendous blessing. To be able to work with a wonderful church brings great happiness. To be able to be associated with godly men who preach, both young and old, is one of the great joys in life.

I'm happy to be a grandfather. I've heard many people say they wish they could have skipped the children and gone straight to the grandchildren. I don't feel that way, because I loved having children in our home, but it sure melts my heart when that little bundle of joy smiles at her Pops!

There are also some things that make me sad. My prayer is that I can do my part to change those things and that the sadness will only be temporary.

I'm sad to see so many hurting families. It is heart breaking to watch couples struggle in their marriage. It is so sad to see parents ignore their children or refuse to teach their children the most important values in life.

I'm sad when people do not turn to the Lord. Many people are hurting, struggling, and generally worn down by life. Jesus said, "Come to me, all who labor and are heavy laden, and I will give you rest" (Matt. 11:28). No life will be perfect, but it can be made so much better by turning to Christ.

I'm sad when Christians walk away from the church. In my life, I have watched way too many Christians leave the church because they got their feelings hurt, because they were disappointed by some leader in the church, because they have become discouraged, or because they think they have found something better. Some have convinced themselves that the church is not relevant, or that the church is unloving, unkind, and uncaring.

I'm sad when preachers are treated unfairly. I hear from a lot of young preachers that are treated in unchristian ways by elders, church members, and others who should be encouraging them. It is discouraging when a man who has committed his life to proclaiming the gospel feels that he can no longer do so because God's people treat him so unfairly.

As you will recognize by now, most of these moments of happiness or sadness are based on external circumstances. My life is filled with an inner joy because Christ is my King and the Lord of my life. He has redeemed me, placed me in his church among some of the greatest people in the world, and promised me a place of eternal rest (1 Pet. 1:3–5).

What makes you happy?

Dear Father up in heaven, thank you for making it possible for us to live a life of joy. Thank you for giving us times when we can be happy so that we can share your love with others. Thank you, dear God, for allowing us to endure moments of sadness so that we can know of your comfort. Help us, Father, to share the joy of being a Christian with as many people as possible. In Jesus' name, Amen.

THIRTY
SECONDS

April 12, 2010

W e understand that faith is one of the key ingredients to our Christian walk. We must have faith if we want to please God (Heb. 11:6). Recently, it was estimated that more than 20,000 people gathered before sunrise to watch Texas Stadium implode. One man who was interviewed said he had been up more than twenty-four hours to attend the big event. The "Super Bowl" ending (as one fan described it) of this Texas landmark was televised on local stations. Texas Stadium was completed in 1971 at a cost of $35 million. At the time, it was the most unique football stadium in the world. It had a hole in the top so that, according to local legend, "God could watch his favorite team."

Compare the cost of the old Texas Stadium to the $1.2 billion price tag for the new Cowboys Stadium. The humongous megatron alone in the new stadium cost more than Texas Stadium. The new massive structure resembles an intergalactic space ship as you make your approach. It has already hosted an NBA All Star game and is scheduled to host next year's Super Bowl, a Final Four, as well as numerous other major events. The new stadium has been dubbed "Jerry-World," "The Jerry-Dome," and one not-so-admiring local sports talk guru called it "The Boss Hogg Bowl." The big discussion now is what will be built on the site of the old stadium.

Did I mentioned the implosion took thirty seconds? Thirty seconds! It got me to thinking, what can happen in thirty seconds? If a massive structure can be destroyed in thirty seconds, what could we do that would be constructive?

In thirty seconds, one could begin to rebuild a broken relationship with those three magic word, "I was wrong," "I am sorry," or "I love you."

In thirty seconds, you can give thanks to God for the numerous ways he has blessed your life.

In thirty seconds, you can say thank you to a friend for sharing their life with you.

In thirty seconds, you can lend a helping hand to an elderly person who is struggling.

In thirty seconds, you can bend your knees to make eye-contact with your child to let them know how much they are loved.

In thirty seconds, you can tell your spouse how much they mean to you and that if you could marry them all over again, you would do it in a heartbeat.

In thirty seconds, you can tell your children that, of all the children in the world, you are thankful that God blessed you with them.

In thirty seconds, you can sing a verse of praise to the Lord.

In thirty seconds, you can read the story of the crucifixion and learn how much God loves you.

In thirty seconds, you can help someone who is less fortunate.

In thirty seconds, you can write someone expressing gratitude and appreciation.

In thirty seconds, you can write a note to encourage a missionary who is doing God's work in some difficult, lonely place in the world.

In thirty seconds, you can tell someone how much God loves them.

In thirty seconds, you can call a loved one just to say, "I love you, and you are in my thoughts and prayers."

In thirty seconds, you can encourage someone who is weak or struggling.

In thirty seconds, you can speak to someone at church who others overlook.

In thirty seconds, you can be kind to someone who seldom receives kindness.

In thirty seconds, you can ask someone to forgive you for the hurt you have brought to their life.

In thirty seconds, you can forgive someone who has wronged you, regardless of whether they have asked you to forgive.

In thirty seconds, you can make a difference in someones life.

In thirty seconds...

Dear God, please help us to use the seconds, minutes, hours, days, and years of our life to bring glory to you. Help us to encourage someone who is hurting. Help us, Father, to realize the great importance of each second of our life. Help us to consider how we treat those around us. Above all, dear Father, please help us to glorify you with every aspect of who we are and to constantly give thanks to you for the indescribable gift of your Son. In his name, Amen.

THE STRENGTH
HE PROVIDES

I t was the best of times, it was the worst of times; it was the age of wisdom, it was the age of foolishness; it was the epoch of belief, it was the epoch of incredulity; it was the season of Light, it was the season of Darkness; it was the spring of hope, it was the winter of despair; we had everything before us, we had nothing before us."

These memorable words, penned by Charles Dickens some 150 years ago, are still relevant in that they certainly describe the current situation in our world. Our nation is facing difficult days economically, morally, and spiritually. Everybody wants to be "bailed out" of their troubles. New philosophies are being expounded which question the foundational blocks that make up our society. We are also seeing those who want to apply these new philosophies to religion. The struggles in religion have found their way into the church of our Lord. Churches are weighing long-held teaching on fundamental subjects such as baptism being essential for the remission of sins, instrumental music in worship, the role of women in the leadership of the church, and fellowship with denominational groups. The apostle Paul must have been referring to the church when he spoke of a time "when people will not endure sound teaching, but having itching ears they will accumulate for themselves teachers to suit their own passions" (2 Tim. 4:3). We are living in that time.

However, let us always remember that it is during these times that God shows himself strong, and his Word shines bright. The history of man proves that in times such as these, and when men come to the end of their rope, they turn to God. People all around us are diligently seeking for something constant. They realize that there is a void in their life. What they do not realize is that it is a God-shaped void that can only be filled by God and his Word. Those who are Christians know that God will strengthen us during these times. We have this knowledge, but sometimes we forget.

The people of God were ready to enter the promise land. They knew it was a land that flowed with milk and honey. They knew that there were giants in the land. They knew that the mighty hand of God would devastate every enemy. They knew that God would care for their every need. Yet they had to be reminded of this.

> Hear, O Israel: you are to cross over the Jordan today, to go in to dispossess nations greater and mightier than you, cities great and fortified up to heaven, a people great and tall, the sons of the Anakim, whom you know, and of whom you have heard it said, 'Who can stand before the sons of Anak?' Know therefore today that he who goes over before you as a consuming fire is the LORD your God. He will destroy them and subdue them before you. So you shall drive them out and make them perish quickly, as the LORD has promised you.
>
> — Deut. 9:1–3

However, as all of us are acutely aware, we sometimes forget what we know. Deuteronomy 8:11 says, "Take care lest you forget the LORD your God by not keeping his commandments and his rules and his statutes, which I command you today." The people of God then, like many of God's people today, had developed spiritual amnesia. Thus, God reminded them. The word *remember* occurs thirteen times in the book of Deuteronomy.

Like God's people of long ago, we are sometimes guilty of forgetting the promises of God. We forget that God has promised us that he will always be with us. We forget that he has promised us that he will not allow any temptation to come into our life that is too great for us to endure (1 Cor. 10:13). We forget that his strength can supply every need we have in our lives (Phil. 4:19). We forget his promise that all things will work out for our good (Rom. 8:28). We forget that we can do all things through him who strengthens us (Phil. 4:13). While we need God's strength each day of our lives, there are various times when we are especially aware of the need for the strength he provides for us.

He provides strength when we are weeping. How do you handle it when you receive word that your only son has been killed while serving his country overseas, when your two-year-old has a brain tumor that cannot be cured, when the doctor tells you that your wife has cancer, when your child you have raised to be faithful to God leaves the church, when your mate of thirty years decides he doesn't love you any more and files for divorce, when you lose your job and your retirement after giving your life to the company, when the congregation your family has been a part of for many years decides to bring in instruments of music, or when you face a myriad of other trials and tribulations of life?

Surely, the apostle Peter recalled the time in his life when he wept bitterly as he wrote these words, "Humble yourselves, therefore, under the mighty hand of God so that at the proper time he may exalt you, casting all your anxieties on him, because he cares for you" (1 Pet. 5:6–7) One family told me they had cried buckets of tears and just did not think they could cry anymore. They confirmed that the only way to get through the weeping brought on by this life is through the strength that God provides.

Even our Savior understood the need for the strength the Father provides when we are weeping. The shortest verse in the pages of Scripture says, "Jesus wept" (John 11:35). A few passages later, Jesus says, "Father, I thank you that you have heard me " (John 11:41). These passages seem to indicate that when Jesus wept, he cried out to the Father. God provided for him the strength he needed when he was weeping. Thank God that this same strength is available to us all.

He provides strength while we wait. Numerous times in my life, I have sat with families anxiously awaiting the results of a surgery of some loved one. Many of us understand what it is like to wait on a child who is making a long drive home from college, news about a job, or some other life-altering event. Isaiah 40:29-31 says, "He gives power to the faint, and to him who has no might he increases strength. Even youths shall faint and be weary, and young men shall fall exhausted; but they who wait for the LORD shall renew their strength; they shall mount up with wings like eagles; they shall run and not be weary; they shall walk and not faint."

The psalmist understood what it is like when we feel we have been attacked, and we are waiting on help from the Lord. Listen to his words as he is waiting on that deliverance.

> The LORD is my light and my salvation; whom shall I fear? The LORD is the stronghold of my life; of whom shall I be afraid? When evildoers assail me to eat up my flesh, my adversaries and foes, it is they who stumble and fall. Though an army encamp against me, my heart shall not fear; though war arise against me, yet I will be confident. One thing have I asked of the LORD, that will I seek after: that I may dwell in the house of the LORD all the days of my life, to gaze upon the beauty of the LORD and to inquire in his temple.
>
> — Psa. 27:1–4

He further described his waiting and the Lord's response in Psa. 40:1–3. "I waited patiently for the LORD; he inclined to me and heard my cry. He drew me up from the pit of destruction, out of the miry bog, and set my feet upon a rock, making my steps secure. He put a new song in my mouth, a song of praise to our God. Many will see and fear, and put their trust in the LORD." May God help us to rely upon Him when we are waiting.

He provides strength when we wrestle with sin. Every child of God is involved in a war with sin and Satan. First Peter 5:8 tells us that the devil "prowls around like a roaring lion, seeking someone to devour." Ephesians 6 teaches us that he has schemes that he will use in warfare against man. He knows our weaknesses, and he will use every means possible to lure us into sin.

However, our God has not left us alone. "No temptation has overtaken you that is not common to man. God is faithful, and he will not let you be tempted beyond your ability, but with the temptation he will also provide the way of escape, that you may be able to endure it" (1 Cor. 10:13). The writer of Hebrews reminds us of the help God provides.

> Since then we have a great high priest who has passed through the heavens, Jesus, the Son of God, let us hold fast our confession. For we do not have a high priest who is unable to sympathize with our weaknesses, but one who in every respect has been tempted as we are, yet without sin. Let us then with confidence draw near to the throne of grace, that we may receive mercy and find grace to help in time of need.
>
> — Heb. 4:14–16

When our High Priest faced temptation, he turned to Scripture. Three times in Luke 4 when Jesus faces the temptations of our adversary, he responded with "It is written…" (Luke 4:4, 8, 12). As with our Lord, we too have a source of strength we can rely on in times of temptation (Psa. 119:9–11).

He provides strength while we work for him. There are times in our lives when working for the Lord can become discouraging. It may become discouraging because of the unkind and negative comments from others. It may become discouraging if we feel that not much is being accomplished. It may become discouraging because of weariness. It is during those times that we should remember that God is with us while we work for him. Paul encouraged the Corinthian Christians by reminding them to be "steadfast, immovable, always abounding in the work of the Lord, knowing that in the Lord your labor is not in vain" (1 Cor. 15:58). Jesus said that a cup of cold water given in his name would not lose its reward (Mark 9:41).

Just as with God's people of old, our successes in the Lord's work will not be accomplished by our strength, our power, our might, our ingenuity, or our educational acumen. It will be accomplished only when we are working in tandem with God. "Finally, be strong in the Lord and in the strength of his might" (Eph. 6:10). Paul knew that what he accomplished came only through the strength he received from above. "I can do all things through him who strengthens me" (Phil. 4:13).

He provides strength as we worship. In our current culture, congregations of God's people are fighting over worship. Some among us have become so entrenched in the culture, they feel everything must be changed. The attitude seems to be, if we have ever done this in the past, it must be discarded. If it is not new, it's bad. There are many who believe God has not spoken about how we should worship him, that he has left it up to us to determine what we think is best. We would plead with our brethren who feel this way, that they not be driven by culture, or by what they feel will be most accepted.

On the other hand, there are those who feel stringently that nothing about our worship assemblies can ever change. The attitude seems to be, if we have never done something a particular way, it cannot be changed. If something is new, it is bad. Many believe that God has told us what genre of songs we must sing or how our worship assembly must be ordered. We would plead with our brethren who feel this way that they not make laws where God has not made laws.

There are passages that we need to consider as we think about worship. "This people honors me with their lips, but their heart is far from me; in vain do they worship me, teaching as doctrines the commandments of men" (Matt. 15:8–9). When Jesus used these Old Testament passages, he was speaking to our minds and hearts. He was saying that we cannot worship God just any way that we choose; that we must use his doctrine, not ours. He was also very clear that it is possible for us to be right doctrinally and still be wrong. If our hearts are not in tune with him, it does not matter how doctrinally correct we may be. Brethren, it is possible to be doctrinally precise and worship with hearts that are on fire. These two do not have to be mutually exclusive. One only needs to read the words recorded by the writer of Psa. 95 to learn that it is possible to worship in such a way that is doctrinally precise, as well as in a way that is joyful, enthusiastic, and filled with anticipation.

When we rely upon the Word of God to guide us in our worship, we will not only do so in a way that is correct, we may see visitors react like they did in 1 Cor. 14:25—"the secrets of his heart are disclosed, and so, falling on his face, he will worship God and declare that God is really among you." We should all be reminded of the words of the wise king from long ago who said, "Trust in the LORD with all your heart, and do not lean on your own understanding. In all your ways acknowledge him, and he will make straight your paths" (Prov. 3:5–6). How arrogant we are when we think we can change his design for worship, either by trying to bring in what we like, even though he has not authorized such, or to bind man-made traditions he has not authorized.

Praise God that we do not have to provide our own strength when we are weeping, waiting, wrestling with sin, working for him, or when we worship. Let all of God's people thank him daily for the strength he provides.

Dear Father, we know that we could not make it through this life without the strength you provide for us. We praise you for the strength you give us at all times in our life. Help us to always be thankful for the strength we have because of Christ. In his name we pray, Amen.

ACKNOWLEDGMENTS

Thank you to Michael Whitworth for presenting me with the cover of this book as a Father's Day gift. This volume would not be in your hands now if Michael had not given me that gift. He challenged me (OK, he prodded me) to allow this book to become a reality. Michael has compiled, edited, created, designed, and published this book. I will forever be thankful for my "adopted son" making this book a reality.

Thank you to my brother, Dale, for his more than gracious and kind *Foreword*. One of the greatest joys in my life is the blessing of working with Dale through The Jenkins Institute. I love our time together each February and at various other times of the year. Dale, one of the greatest blessings in my life is to be known as your brother. I love you dearly.

It is also important for me to express my deep gratitude to every person who has read the "Thoughts from the Mound" blog. Thank you for your words of encouragement. Thank you for sharing the posts with others. Thank you for your love for the Lord and your desire to grow closer to him.

Our appreciation for the people who make up the Lewisville Church of Christ is immense. Thank you for allowing me to stand in your presence each week to proclaim the unsearchable riches of Christ. Thank you for your love for the Word of God. Thank you for your encouragement, your example, and your friendship. We love you all.

36680310R00115

Made in the USA
San Bernardino, CA
30 July 2016